Reiki
A Path to Freedom

Unlock the true potential of
your Reiki tools

Elaine Hamilton Grundy

Disclaimer

This publication contains the opinions and ideas of its author. It is intended to provide helpful and informative material on the subjects addressed in the publication. It is sold with the understanding that the author and publisher are not engaged in rendering medical, psychological, or any other kind of professional services in the book. The reader should consult his or her medical, psychological, or other competent professional before adopting any of the suggestions in this book or drawing inferences from it.

The author and publisher specifically disclaim all responsibility for any liability, loss, or risk, personal or otherwise, that is incurred as a consequence, either directly or indirectly, of the use and application of any of the contents of this book.

Copyright ©2019 Elaine Hamilton Grundy. All rights reserved. No part of this publication may be reproduced, distributed, or transmitted in any form or by any means, electronic or mechanical, without prior written permission from the publisher. For permission, contact the author at the website below.

Publisher: The Reiki Centre Pte Ltd, Singapore
Website: www.Reiki-Centre.com

All rights reserved. No part of this book may be reproduced, scanned, or distributed in any printed or electronic form without permission of the publisher.

ISBN: 978-1-6937641-7-2
1. Reiki (Healing system). 2. Alternative medicine. 3. Integrative medicine

Book Designer: Justine Elliott

To my students

Reiki
A Path to Freedom

CONTENTS

Learning to Unlearn 9
Introduction 15

Chapter 1: Universal Life Force 25
Reiki and Our Perceptions of Reiki 26
Take Your Experiences above Your Theories 29
The Evolution of Our Viewpoint of Reiki 29
What Is Reiki? 32
Is Reiki Intelligent? 32
Life's Purpose 33
Dismantling Our Belief Systems 34
A Little Story 36
Coming into Your Own Truth 38

Chapter 2: A Finger Pointing to the Moon 39
  Is Your Reiki Practice Self-Empowering? 40
  Reiki Hands-on Self-Treatment 41
  Breaking Free of Rules 42
  Respect Everything You're Been Taught, and Hold It Lightly 46
  Rules Should Hold You to a Higher Integrity 47

Chapter 3: Understanding the Reiki Symbols 49
Understanding Symbology 50
The Symbol Advantage 52
The Power Symbol 54
The Harmony Symbol 56
The Connection (Sending) Symbol 58

Chapter 4: Reiki Attunements for Personal Growth .. 61
The Master Symbol 62
The Importance of Lineage 63
Attuning to Universal Flow 65

Chapter 5: Reiki as a Spiritual Practice 69
What Is a Spiritual Practice? 72
Me Before You 74
"Me First," as Service to Others 77

Chapter 6: Turning Attention Inwards 85
The Answers Are Within Us 87
Why Is Self-Treatment So Important? 89
Commitment to Our Inner World 91
Be Alert to the Process 94
Getting Comfortable with Uncomfortable Feelings 96
Accept, Accept, Accept 98
Nothing to Fix or Change 100
Sincerity and Ego 101
Being Willing to See Where You Are 104
Beware of Skipping Stages of Spiritual
Development 104

Chapter 7: Deconditioning the Mind 107
Sending Reiki as a Spiritual Contemplation 108
Aligning Your Intention to the Correct
Outcome 110
Timing Is Everything 111
It's Not in Your Best Interest 112
Use Reiki Sending as a Navigational Tool 115
Sending to Resistance 116
Sending to Difficult Relationships 118
Working with Negative Emotions 122
Sending to Affirmations 124
Working on Ourselves, Not Others 127
Clearing the Path 129

Chapter 8: Minding the Gap 131
   Spacious Awareness..134
   Doorways into Our True Self..........................136
   Everything Is Welcome.....................................138
   The Paradox of Freedom.................................140
   Life Loves Living Life 142
   Choose Your Focal Point..................................144

Chapter 9: Living Life's Purpose......................... 147
   The Creative Impulse..148
   What Is Life's Purpose? 150
   Life Purpose or Ego Agenda?.............................153
   Shine Your Big, Bright Light...............................156
   Building on What You Were Given 158
   The Co-Creative Process 159

Chapter 10: In the End 163
   Postlude: Next Steps...167
   Acknowledgements...170

Prelude

Learning to Unlearn

"The only thing worth learning is to unlearn. The way to do this is to question everything you think you know."

—Byron Katie

The truth is not what you think it is. Everything we think we know is learned, and all this learning has formed layers upon layers of opinions and beliefs over our original truth. So, what happens when we unlearn? What happens when we question everything that we think we know? The answer is quite simple: We stand in the truth of our own experience. And this truth may be a very different one to the one you are currently projecting onto your life.

This book invites you to begin an unlearning process. To question your version of truth and look for what lies beneath and behind your assumptions and beliefs.

From the moment we become aware of the wider world as children, we are taught to deny, dismiss, or change our truth. We are told to stop crying when we feel sad. We are taught we should be doing this rather than that. We are taught to think about others before ourselves (not to be "selfish"). We are taught to say nice things and trust our elders.

Of course, socialisation has its place, but it also deadens us. Every layer of falseness is another dampening of our inner truth. By the time we are adults, there is such a huge chasm between our genuine truth and what we falsely believe our truth to be that a vague unease, dissatisfaction, and sadness permeate our thoughts and actions. We usually misinterpret the source of this discomfort—as we misinterpret just about everything by then—as something that needs fixing, such as our job, our relationships, our finances, or our environment, or as something about us (thinking we're "not good enough" is common). But what if all we really need to do is to unlearn everything that we think we know and look again with clear eyes?

In this book, I describe the Reiki spiritual journey from my personal perspective as a person who was at one time deeply disconnected from my inner truth and then reclaimed it using Reiki. Originally, I was so focused on my search for connection that I failed to realise I already had what I sought. I was convinced that the answers lay outside of myself—in a teacher, a healing technique, a fantastic book. This is what we are taught after all: that other people know what we should do. But as I consistently worked on myself doing daily self-treatments incorporating Reiki symbols and attunements, I grasped the understanding that unlearning was more liberating than learning. I grasped that questioning everything I thought I knew brought freedom. And surprisingly to me, the less opinions I held, the happier I felt.

The aim of this book is to invite you to see that all you need is already in you. You can find your freedom and happiness through the beautiful process of your Reiki practice. Reiki also provides a path for self-healing that opens the way to deep self-awareness. Using your Reiki tools will allow you many opportunities to uncover your inner truth.

The spiritual journey is an inward-focused endeavour that does not depend on dogma or philosophy. It is an experience—of knowing yourself as a unique expression of life. No one else can give you that; nor can anyone tell you who you are and what you were born to do. You must discover your essence for yourself. However, pathways and tools can be useful, especially if you feel that you have lost touch with your truth.

When I say truth, I mean the subjective truth of your personal experience.

We are all journeying to "find ourselves" even though we cannot be lost. How could we lose ourselves? Yet for many of us it feels as if we have. We feel lost and intuitively know that a deeper connection is possible. We also intuitively know that we are navigating our lives according to someone else's set of rules—or at least that was my strong sense when I started on my own journey of personal discovery.

Spiritual paths are useful guiding points, and by my definition, must originate from an enlightened master, someone who illuminates the way for the rest of us. This is important: The tour guide needs to know the destination. Paradoxically the destination is inner truth, so another person cannot know how you can get there for yourself, as everyone's journey is different, but one person's journey into inner truth can at least help provide general pointers for others to follow. That at least is the starting point assumption: Someone else who has discovered his or her inner truth is a better guide than someone who hasn't.

My belief is that this was the case for Mikao Usui (1865–1926), the founder of the Reiki path I learned. Today I tread the path he laid down for us and I feel that the more of us who travel it, the easier and better defined it becomes for others. We explore this path together, though ultimately, each of us walks it in a different way.

All Reiki students have been called to the same path. When life force calls you, it is inviting you home. With the first attunement, you are initiated into the journey. When they think back to it, many students of Reiki will say that a switch clicked, and something in them knew the significance of what had just happened. You may not have consciously realized this was occurring and you may only be reading this book out of curiosity, nonetheless, the switch has been clicked on and somewhere, deep inside, your truth is arising in your awareness and attempting to capture your attention.

You may or may not be a Reiki master yet. Perhaps you have only just started your Reiki journey, and you are curious as to what the other levels of mastery hold for you. I hope this book inspires you to keep exploring and experiencing. Although much of the book talks about tools you may not have yet encountered, Reiki's spiritual path is still relevant. Take the core message from my description and apply it to whatever level of Reiki you are at; self-treatment is equally valid to take you to a deep state of connection within yourself even without Level 2 and Level 3 tools. This pathway is deeply significant for you simply because you have been attuned into it. How far you travel with Reiki and how consciously you utilise the tools is totally up to you but I hope this book resonates with you and wakes up a part of you that has always known the significance of your initial attraction to Reiki. It is no accident.

Learning to unlearn is the key principle of this book. Take off the many layers of conditioning, of education, of societal expectations, of cultural norms, and of ancestral baggage and stand in the light of who you really are. Only you can do this. When you realise you are responsible for your own freedom and happiness, it is empowering and sobering. Now there are no excuses. You and you alone must navigate your life.

Thankfully, we have Reiki. This beautiful, loving energy gently accompanies us, not as a guide or soothsayer, but as a source of courage, vitality, and inspiration.

With Reiki, you can get in touch with the supportive benevolence of the universe. Universal life force always has your back, not in an "everything will work out great" way, but simply, fully, unconditionally. You are supported, even when things around you are falling apart. Once you sense this, you can fully participate in your life, and shine your light into the world with confidence and an abiding sense of safety and belonging.

Your personal journey also has impact globally. It only takes one or two per cent of any population to shift the entire population's collective consciousness. If you are the only one on a spiritual path in your family, in your community, or in your friendship group, that is fine. You can make a difference that is noticeable and appreciated. With or without the support of your cohort, make the journey. We all must make this journey alone anyway.

You must be willing and ready to shift your consciousness first—this is the primary term and condition of your personal freedom. In the sense that any spiritual journey is a personal endeavour your Reiki path is your very own hero's journey. But there is also a very real impact that your own inner discovery has on others. Your personal freedom will affect others in a profound way. When you navigate your life with love and compassion, you impact all those around you.

Reiki began as a spiritual path and we are all being called back to this path. In Usui's time there were thousands attracted to his call, now there are many millions. Imagine the global impact we could have if we all paid heed to the calling.

Introduction

"It's all an inside job. It's all something we do to ourselves – mistakenly, unknowingly, and oftentimes unconsciously"

—Adyashanti

This book assumes that you have a yearning to empower yourself and look deeply into your own experience to find your truth. It assumes you have been initiated into Reiki and feel a connection or curiosity that makes you want to journey further.

Over the past twenty-five years of using Reiki, I have moved through my own journey of discovery. In the beginning, I saw Reiki as a wonder cure, and I easily gave my power away to the belief that "everything will be fixed" by Reiki. This approach worked well for me for years. My life and health improved significantly, and my belief that Reiki would take care of everything was a perfect container in which to dump all my issues and personal problems.

But after a few years, I hit a natural barrier. I noticed that after the initial release of unhealthy behaviours and patterns, the deeper ones still weren't shifting. My most toxic behaviours and ingrained issues didn't want to go into the Reiki container. At that point, I did as many others do. I began to search for alternatives to Reiki—other healing modalities.

Alongside this impulse to search for answers, I am fortunate that my commitment to my Reiki practice never wavered. I travelled all around the world, going to workshops and learning diverse ways of healing, finding new answers, and deepening my self-awareness. Every day I would do my Reiki self-treatment, I would use my symbols, I would attune others to Reiki. And yet every day, I would also go out seeking and looking—asking: *Where is my inner peace? How can I find my freedom from all this inner angst and suffering?*

Then one day, out of nowhere, it dawned on me: *Reiki is my spiritual practice. It is what I have been seeking. It has always been here. It has never been absent.*

I hope this book is your shortcut to actively engage in a path it took me many years to recognise. The answers to your inner angst are within you, everything you need is already present in your Reiki toolbox.

How This Book Is Organised

The book has a simple, two-part structure. In Part I, I lay out the foundational elements of Reiki that make it suitable as a path for spiritual development. In Part II, I describe the four stages of transformation of consciousness that a long-term, ongoing Reiki practice facilitates.

We begin the book in Chapter 1, "Universal Life Force," by exploring a broader meaning of Reiki. We need to be willing to admit we really cannot understand what Reiki truly is because with Reiki we're dealing with both *relative* and *absolute* reality. The paradox is that these viewpoints co-exist and yet we cannot always see them both at the same time. The absolute and relative are essentially flip sides of the same coin.

You will notice that when I talk about Reiki, often I am explaining it from a *relative* viewpoint—in other words, with me/you and Reiki as separate "entities." I do this because it is part of the evolution of our relationship with Reiki. Practice tends to begin for most of us as a feeling that there is a movement of an external energy, which we feel coming through our hands, from the "outside" to the "inside" of our bodies.

As we progress along the Reiki path, we begin to intuitively grasp, and also viscerally experience, that universal life force includes us—which is why it is termed *universal*. From the *absolute* viewpoint, Reiki is not outside us. It *is* us, and it is everything else as well.

At the beginning of our spiritual journey, this *absolute* viewpoint may seem nonsensical, and even is often unhelpful. There are stages of spiritual maturation we must go through, realisations we must have about our true nature, before it all begins to make sense.

Perhaps it already makes sense, and you recognise the process I describe.

Perhaps it sounds like nonsense. And if so, I ask that you persevere and remain curious, as exploring what Reiki is can be as rich and rewarding an exploration as exploring your inner life.

In Chapter 2, "A Finger Pointing to the Moon," the book will move on to a discussion of Reiki education. There is such a vast range of styles of Reiki teaching, techniques, and opinions that it can be very hard to discern what is "correct." I invite you to examine your Reiki education and the rules and regulations surrounding your Reiki practice to see if they are serving *you* correctly *for you*. Inner truth is not conditioned by rules, and the first step in reclaiming your power and freedom is to follow your path with ease. Life on your own terms is effortless and natural.

Exploring the spiritual path suggested in this book will be impossible for you if you are lumbered with rules and disempowering beliefs. Decide which parts of your Reiki practice are serving you, and which you can allow to fall away. Learning to unlearn also means questioning the spiritual tools themselves.

In Chapter 3, "The Reiki Symbols," my aim is to deepen your understanding of why and how the symbols work and to encourage your experimentation and personal exploration. The symbols are like gateways to information. This information supports us in ways we may not have learnt to do for ourselves. They allow us to fully resonate with the yang/yin qualities of power and harmony, and they allow us to make a deeper connection with what we want in life.

The final tool to explore is the attunement process. In Chapter 4, "Attunements for Personal Growth," I outline my experience of what an attunement is, and how we can utilise this transformative initiation to gain a direct experience of *absolute* reality. A lot of the students in my Reiki workshops and training programs are fascinated to learn that I regularly attune myself. I do not reserve this ritual action purely for the benefit of other people.

An attunement is your doorway into universal life force. Attunements are not only used for activating Reiki in others. More profoundly, they are for attuning yourself to yourself.

By Chapter 5, "Reiki as a Spiritual Practice," we are ready to investigate spirituality. What am I referring to when I call Reiki a *spiritual path*? In short, I explore the importance of focusing attention within in order to shine more brightly.

The English word *spirit* comes from the Latin root *spiritus*, which means "breath" or "air," which is the animating force of our bodies. For the purposes of this book, we will assume the word to mean "animating or vital principle." And our enquiry will be: What is this vital principle within me?

Through Reiki practice, we come into intimate contact with our inner vitality. Uncovering and exploring this light is our spiritual journey.

In Part II, "The Reiki Spiritual Path," I describe four stages of inner exploration. Each stage is outlined with a level of Reiki education in mind, but the path is not in any way intended to be exclusive to Reiki masters. The spiritual path is open to everyone, no matter the level of Reiki training we have, and we can use Reiki with mindfulness at any stage, using whichever tools we have been taught.

Throughout the book I refer to students of Reiki simply as *Reiki students*. Although I was taught the term *Reiki practitioner*, I understand it can now be confused with those who practise Reiki as a professional therapeutic practice. To avoid confusion the term *Reiki student* means all of us who use Reiki as a method of self-practice—we are all essentially "students of Reiki."

Most of us start our Reiki journeys completely unaware of our inner potential for self-healing. Thus, the shift in Reiki Level 1, from a disempowered state to possessing basic ability in self-healing, is groundbreaking. This ability forms the foundation of our Reiki journey: consistent Reiki self-treatment. Routine practice directs our attention inwards and balances our energy so that we can gain courage for inwards journeying.

Chapter 6, "Turning Attention Inwards," is the first critical part of beginning a spiritual journey. We must see the importance of looking inwards for answers instead of out in the world. Turning attention inwards is the realisation that our body has an innate wisdom, and then actively working to develop our sensitivity to this wisdom. This is the first task towards residing fully in our natural home. For many of us, it is a difficult and challenging process to become willing to listen to the body; but its rewards are great. Once you fully inhabit your body, you can more easily discern your inner truth and are much less likely to be influenced or swept away by others' needs, wants, or demands.

As we get more in touch with the inner wisdom of the body, we begin to see the mass of constricted and confusing thoughts that appear to rule our inner world. Our conditioned egos have very fixed views on how life should or shouldn't be going. If resistance forms around the way life *is* going, we suffer terribly. In Chapter 7, "Deconditioning the Mind," we'll discuss the spiritual stage of coming into balance with your life and not fighting against what is. This stage coincides with, but is not exclusive to, the Reiki Level 2 training, where symbols are introduced. The use of symbols opens us to a wider perspective. We begin to see all our conditioning and restrictive thoughts; and sending Reiki to these helps us see our resistance and release it. At this stage we also begin to see our inner light and cultivate it by orienting ourselves towards our values and priorities.

In Chapter 8, "Minding the Gap," I discuss how when we are fully residing in the body, and our minds are more open and quieter, we notice a deep and peaceful presence or awareness. The next stage of the journey is the *absolute* experience of Reiki. This is a paradigm shift in our spiritual development, the period when we see that "me" and "Reiki" are actually one and the same source. During this phase we become more curious about the gaps in our thinking process, and more acquainted with the awareness that fills us, with consistent and all-encompassing presence.

We conclude our survey of the stages of spiritual development with Chapter 9, "Living Life's Purpose." We feel the impulse of life's flow and sense where it wants to go. We begin to correctly identify that this impulse is not an egoic grasping to fill a void within us, but life itself bursting out of us. At this stage, Reiki students typically find they have passion and creative enthusiasm that brings abundance and joy. When we work with this impulse correctly, amazing things begin to happen. Life meets us fully, and we experience what has always been available to us: unconditional love, support, and purpose.

Chapter 10, "In the End," offers a summary of the four stages and the way we shift our perspective. There are profound shifts as we journey through and yet surprisingly life retains much of its same qualities, the same experiences present themselves but without the suffering. Freedom comes to us when we fully align with what life is giving us, living life on purpose and willingly. I also provide a prelude of tips and next steps for your own Reiki practice. Simple additions to add to your daily routine that will give new depth and clarity to your journey.

Cycling Deeper and Deeper

The stages of the spiritual journey outlined in Part II of this book follow a flow that comes with mastery. In my own personal experience, mastering each level takes decades; it is still a work in progress.

This book is an invitation to slow down, be honest with yourself, and go back over the basics, again and again. Building strong foundations is essential to achieving the freedom you seek. Shortcuts lead to misunderstandings, and at every opportunity, our pesky egos will delude us into thinking that our knowledge is complete, and we are ready to move on. Whereas in truth, nothing is ever "completed." We must continually revisit and re-examine. The spiritual journey of Reiki is like a spiral, cycling us deeper and deeper, as we find ourselves coming closer and closer to our inner freedom.

To illustrate this, let me give you an example from my own story.

Ever since I was very young, I have been a people-pleaser. I was the child every parent wanted: I was studious, organised, and polite, and I did my chores without complaint. I did everything I could to win my parents' approval, and when I got praise and positive attention, I moved that strategy on to friends and colleagues. But I realised that by putting other people's happiness before my own I was moving further from my own truth.

Using Reiki, I began to grow in confidence and clarity. With extra energy and courage, during my first Reiki spiral I practised the art of saying no. Many people didn't like it, and why would they? The obedient child was suddenly rebelling. Friends said they liked me better before I started doing all this "'Reiki stuff," and some dropped away, as I was no longer fulfilling my role as their doormat.

At the time of these loses, it was very painful, and I questioned my resolve: Wasn't it better to have more friends? Were they right? Was I nicer and better before all this started?

But I also noticed that the more empowered I became, the more energised and happier I was. No longer burdened by everyone else's expectations and demands, I had more time for myself and for things that brought me joy. I found a new group of friends who appreciated me for who I was and didn't make unfair demands of me.

But at work things were still abysmal!

So, in the next cycle of breaking my people-pleaser habit, I began to be more assertive at work. I had been emboldened by the success and positive results of saying no at a social level, so this time, it was easier to say no at work. The method was already tried and tested, and I had much less self-doubt. It was still tough for me and people still didn't like it, but I had more confidence.

This spiral of saying no continues to go around and around in my life as I tackle things closer and closer to my heart. As I continue to work, for example, on family relationships, I am hitting on core beliefs that began the behaviour patterns I would like to heal in the first place: deeply ingrained fears that disobedience will result in withdrawal of love or in me hurting those I love. Each cycle of practice has given me an opportunity to go deeper in my exploration and be more open to the vulnerable and sometimes painful emotions the spiritual journey brings up.

Many deep issues present themselves like this. Spiritual maturation is not just one cycle and we're done. We can be hit time and time again with issues we thought we had resolved. It's normal that as we remove one layer of false beliefs and fears the next appears. Nothing has gone wrong, we haven't failed or missed something. It's simply the next layer. The fact that an issue raises its head again means we're not quite finished healing.

Life will keep reminding us what is still to be resolved—that's the wonderful thing about it. As the Reiki spiral deepens, so our trust grows. We fear the outcome less and less, because the more we release our resistance, the more we flow and the better it gets. If we stop thinking of our issues as something to fix and see them more like layers of resistance to gently unpeel, then we begin to work with life. Life shows us what's next, and we cooperate.

Eventually, we see that the whole thing is a dance. Life flows and we respond with cooperation or resistance, and this creates the next flow—a subtle and paradoxical merging of our will with the universal will.

Full cooperation equals freedom.

Resistance equals suffering.

PART I
The Foundations of Reiki

1.
Universal Life Force

The "paradox" is only a conflict between reality and your feeling of what reality "ought to be."
—Richard Feynman

One of the hardest things for the human mind to do is to stay curious. The way the conscious and subconscious minds interact is a testament to this. In order to function in our lives, we need to filter things. Thousands of thoughts cross our mind daily, and without a mental filtering mechanism, we would be lost in a sea of confusion. This filtering mechanism is regulated by the subconscious mind. It notices what we like and dislike, and like a Google algorithm, it builds our preferences and installs "cookies." Unlike with real computer browsers, however, it's not easy to clear the cache of the mind. As a result, after years the subconscious mind slows everything down. It becomes more difficult to search outside of our usual parameters and we gradually close off to new ideas and opportunities. Our responses become thoroughly conditioned and we mistake our conditioning for our truth. Much like advertising algorithms we begin to only see what our subconscious filters think we want to see, and so our lives begin to take on self-fulfilling and increasingly ridged parameters of beliefs.

The core issue we face in finding our own inner truth is our conditioning, particularly due to an aspect of our mental functioning that I term *ego*. If we begin to see the ego as simply the conditions and preferences we have subconsciously set over the years, it helps to loosen the hold we have on the idea: "The ego is me."

We will discuss this idea in more detail later. For now, just lightly hold onto this inaccurate idea that you already know yourself and be curious. What if what you thought of as "me" was in fact just a Google algorithm? And what if after you cleared your cache you could not only see your life with fresh eyes but also come into the fullness of your true being?

With curiosity, look at Reiki with fresh eyes too—from a perspective not based on what I am saying, but on your actual experience. Use this sense of curiosity throughout this book; see if you can set aside any preconceived ideas or beliefs you may have about Reiki and how to practice it. Test everything I am saying, not against your own opinions, but against your actual experience.

My hope is that you will be using your own practice as a big experiment during the reading of this book, and that if what you are reading doesn't ring true for you at any point, you'll discover what else does. If you were to toss out all your pre-existing knowledge of Reiki and started anew, what might you discover for yourself?

Reiki and Our Perceptions of Reiki

When I learned Reiki and was told that it was a Japanese term meaning "universal life force," I remember thinking, *Cool!* I didn't give it much further thought. I felt heat and tingling in my hands that first day in class and was delighted by the experience. I had no doubt something significant was happening. When I did my self-treatment, I felt relaxed, calm, and peaceful.

Years went by, and I continued to think it was wonderful to tap into universal life force, to have this limitless supply of energy at my beck and call. This is exactly how my early experience felt. I would self-treat (fuel up), and then off I'd go again. Along the way, I noticed various insecurities, fears, beliefs, and physical and emotional toxicity dropping away. I attributed my transformation to Reiki. Reiki rocked!

I was told that Reiki was an external energy and I was pulling it in through my hands during treatment and filling myself up. Because this was how it felt, I didn't question the explanation. I also didn't question any philosophical information I was given. The experience of Reiki matched my beliefs around Reiki.

During challenging times, I felt grateful to Reiki for sustaining me and helping me get through the day. I relied on Reiki in many ways. For example: I suffered from frequent insomnia starting at a young age. Due to my ability to self-treat, I felt much more secure knowing that I would be able to cope perfectly well even after a sleepless night. Reiki felt like a security blanket or guardian angel. Ten years after being attuned, I still saw Reiki as an *external* source of energy, as something different from me.

My shifting relationship with Reiki came hand in hand with a deepening search for inner peace. I searched for many years, always looking for answers outside me. I talked about self-empowerment, but what I really wanted was to boost my self-esteem and feel more confident. Although I noticed that my fine work with Reiki was developing my personality and shifting my negative beliefs into positive beliefs, I also could see that it was not shifting the deeper feelings of dissatisfaction bubbling under the surface of my life.

To an outsider, it would have seemed like I had everything: a thriving Reiki practice, a healthy, happy family, a wonderful home, and even a great relationship with my parents! Yet, underneath it all, I was discontented.

This slow-dawning realisation was both liberating and depressing—liberating in that I knew it called for a radical change in my strategy, depressing in that I really didn't know what to do next.

During this time, my relationship with Reiki began to change. I noticed that we were beginning to merge. Sometimes when I did a self-treatment, I couldn't really tell where my hands, my body, and the air met. Everything had a feeling of oneness. I experienced a very intense vibration, and it was as though I could feel and hear the cosmos on a molecular level. At one point, I mentally travelled into the cells themselves, where I could see their microscopic contents moving and merging, and otherwise going about their business. It was bizarre, to say the least! From having a series of such experiences, I began to open to the possibility that I really didn't know Reiki well at all, and I considered for the first time that perhaps Reiki and I were one and the same thing.

My focus went in an entirely new direction. During my self-treatments, I spent more time exploring the feeling of oneness. In the past, I had come to Reiki to give me energy, like an exhausted warrior returning home to rest before setting out on another gruelling quest. It had never yet occurred to me to explore the self-treatment itself as a spiritual practice because I thought the main purposes for Reiki were to reduce my stress and fuel my activities. But when I shifted my focus and started travelling inwards, I realised that what I was looking for was under my nose all along. The more I explored the idea and the experience of oneness, the more peaceful I felt. The more I saw my self-treatment as a spiritual practice, the more connected to my truth I became.

Did you know that our perceptions change as we evolve spiritually? Noticing and being curious about these shifts allows us to keep moving and not get stuck in our algorithms and expectations. Curiosity is the key to self-treatment. We so often ignore the reality of our own experience, especially if it doesn't match up with our theories and expectations, but we don't have to. Take a few moments now to reflect: How do you see your self-treatments? Are they a means to an end—to get something out of it—or are they the end itself?

Take Your Experiences above Your Theories

Take time to notice the qualities of your personal experiences with Reiki, and of the deep places you go inside. I have noticed that sometimes I experience intense heat and vibrations, out-of-body travel, an expansive sense of merging with the cosmos, and other weird and wonderful things. But sometimes I experience nothing except my own overactive mind frustratingly spinning its wheels and refusing to stop.

Reiki self-treatment is a practice of openness, an opportunity simply to see what arises and be OK with it. A chance to be curious and enjoy the moment without resisting it.

During your next self-treatment, pause and notice:
What is the experience you are having?
Is anything opening for you?

When you come to self-treatment from a stance of curiosity rather than preconceived ideas, the truth can emerge from the experience. My experience with heat or tingling is the truth. My opinion of *why* it is like that may be fiction. When I allow the truth of my experience to be enough, then the *why* will emerge if it needs to. And when we know something deeply, from direct experience of it, we do not need anyone else to validate our knowledge or agree with us about what it means.

This is what inner truth is: a deep knowing grounded in experience, rather than opinions. In this way, every time your experience changes—as it almost always will—you can evolve with it and not get stuck in the past.

The Evolution of Our Viewpoint of Reiki

At the beginning of the Reiki journey, we see Reiki as something outside us. This is the *relative viewpoint*. In Level 1 classes, Reiki is discussed as an energy that is separate and different from us—coming into our body to harmonise and balance us. We feel it in our hands or perhaps entering us through the crown or heart centre. It feels as if it is an extra something that wasn't there before the first attunement we received.

This way of imparting the information to us is appropriate. In learning any subject, layers of information must be absorbed. There is no point trying to teach a primary school student quantum mechanics. First, introduce the concept of matter, then atoms, and only then, subatomic physics. And so it is for Reiki instruction. First, we teach our students the concept of universal life force, and then they test it.

Does it work for them? Do they see benefits? If yes, they may go on to Reiki Level 2, where this instruction is taken a step further through incorporating symbols in their healing practices. This requires them to make a huge leap of imagination, which is soon followed by the experience of sending Reiki through time and space—*distance healing.*

They then test this concept. Does sending Reiki work for them? Students must discern if it does for themselves. *If I apply the symbols to my life, can I see a positive difference?* If yes, they may move on to Reiki Level 3, where a huge energy shift is offered through instruction in giving the attunement process.

From the point of view of the student, at every level of Reiki training comes new insight, a new way of looking at Reiki that matches both the level of education we are receiving and our openness to the information, which is partly based on our experience of the level of knowledge and skill we mastered before.

The hope of the instructor is that we students are, in fact, curious and developing our opinions—that we are not static and stuck in what the teacher told us at Level 1.

As you read this book, you may change your view of the different stages of Reiki practice. From my own experience in teaching, it is evident to me that the committed student's perception of Reiki will change over time and become less relative.

Contemporary physicists understand that there is a way fields behave on the level of matter and a paradoxical way that fields behave at the quantum level—and both ways are coexisting. Both are part of our reality. The predictable field of matter and the multi-possibility of the quantum field overlap.

There is a seeming paradox in Reiki because it can appear to the student as both *relative* ("me" and "Reiki" are separate entities), and *absolute* ("me" and "Reiki' are one and the same energy). The *absolute viewpoint* regarding Reiki appears with experience, as we continue to deepen our relationship with it. Sometimes we can perceive that Reiki is not just coming through our hands. It is present everywhere. It is quantum.

You may have heard Reiki teachers talk about *embodying* or *becoming* Reiki. This is a reference to the experience of merging our sensations into the room or with our clients. In self-treatments, when we're embodying Reiki, we sometimes have the feeling that we can't distinguish between our hands and where they touch our body. At this level of experience, we may feel tingling or subtle vibrations throughout the body, like all our cells are resonating with one another and the environment around us.

If we express curiosity about these sensations, without interpreting them through the lens of our existing beliefs about Reiki, what are they telling us?

When it happens to you, your mind may tell you that the merging sensation is your imagination— "just a trick of the mind." (That's funny, isn't it, the mind telling you that it's playing tricks on you?) But if you let drop these sceptical thoughts and stay with your direct experience of how you feel, you will enter a deeper truth and know that what you are sensing is the absolute viewpoint: *Me and Reiki are one. My life force and universal life force is the same life force.*

I invite you to accept the simple reality of whatever occurs when you practice Reiki. And to investigate what Reiki is from a stance of open curiosity. This is an investigation into universal life force itself, the infinite vastness of life, which is as much within us as it is in the entire cosmos.

What Is Reiki?

In Japanese, the word *Reiki* means "universal life force." The energy is understood to be all-encompassing, as it is the vital spark or evolutionary force that is demonstrated in the nature that we see all around us. It exists beyond human conditions, beyond right and wrong, beyond rules and regulations, beyond beliefs.

When we investigate its quality as we do our Reiki self-treatments or treat people and come into deep communion with Reiki, what else is present?

When I "Reiki" myself—*Reiki* being my shorthand expression for *giving a Reiki treatment to*—I feel a deep sense of awareness. Life force is not without substance. Sometimes it feels deeply loving and supportive, sometimes it feels powerful, sometimes very gentle. It really is a total mystery.

Your knowledge of Reiki will come from direct experience and is best grounded in your personal truth. Inquire: When you Reiki yourself, do you feel a quality of presence or awareness?

As we explore the mystery, it is useful to contemplate what Reiki is. From an *absolute* viewpoint, if we and Reiki are the same, then this exploration into the mystery of Reiki will also shed light onto our own inner truth of who we ultimately are.

All too often, Reiki students come to a definition of Reiki that feels comfortable and then leave it at that. Without ongoing curiosity our practice becomes static and limited, we make assumptions about what Reiki can and can't do for us and then never challenge or explore these assumptions further. If you are a teacher this is a recipe for stagnation, Reiki is evolving as much as we are. Universal life force doesn't stand still. What Reiki was one hundred years ago in Usui's time is not what Reiki is today, as shocking as that may be to contemplate.

Is Reiki Intelligent?

This question can open a lot of debate in Reiki circles. Many students believe that Reiki is intelligent and therefore will know where to go in your body, and in effect, you need do nothing but show up.

There is truth to this when you look at Reiki from an *absolute* viewpoint—that you and Reiki and life are one and the same source, so yes, you/Reiki/life is/are intelligent. But in the beginning, you could misinterpret this to mean that Reiki, as energy separate from and more intelligent than you, knows what to do; ergo, you might just abdicate responsibility for yourself. Unless you can fully understand the truth of the idea that "'I/Reiki/life is/are one source," this belief that Reiki is (more) intelligent is not particularly helpful.

It is more helpful to consider Reiki an evolving awareness that sparks life. Nature, evolution, the expansion of the cosmos—this is life force in action, and we are part of this inevitable process.

If, when we personalise the idea of Reiki as intelligent, we think that this means "Reiki will solve all my problems," then we are misinterpreting what it really means.

Reiki is universal life force that's evolving to know itself. This is an evolutionary impulse in all of us that guides our spiritual journey. We all have this impulse. You could call it your life purpose. Ironically, we are usually first drawn into our spiritual journey by personalising and misinterpreting the evolutionary impulse as a search for our individual purpose or meaning. The "punchline" at the end of the journey is your realisation that your personal journey is not personal to you at all—in fact, you are being called by Reiki.

Life's Purpose

When I was younger, I was searching ceaselessly for my life purpose, so I spent ridiculous amounts of money attending "Passion and Purpose" workshops. These types of workshops have their place and can be important opportunities to journey inwards and find your truth, but for most of us, they are misinterpreted by the ego as something we should be doing: "designing" our purpose.

Life purpose is simply following life's flow, rather than your ego's agenda. When I say you are being *called* by Reiki, I am referring to Reiki as universal life force. Life is calling you to a deeper appreciation of your own life force. The deep spiritual question "Who am I?" is being asked at all levels because your personal ego, your deeper inner truth, and the entire life force wants to know the answer.

Left to its own devices, what the ego wants and pursues is recognition and achievement—because it is conditioned that way. That's also society's algorithm for us. But these are false purposes that can never bring us lasting happiness.

I'm sure you know this already.

The problem, when we misinterpret our life purpose, is that we fail to see the opportunity, growth, and reality of what life is trying to show us in every moment. All our false beliefs end up distracting us and trapping us in mind games of asking, *Why this?* and *Why that?* Meanwhile, life continues to flourish and evolve in its own quest of the bigger "Who am I?" and we are missing out on this gift.

If we insist on aligning ourselves with our ego's objectives, we will find ourselves largely disappointed and frequently exhausted.

Your life purpose is not some magnificent achievement your ego has designed and wants from life. When you come into the truth of who you really are then your real purpose emerges, it comes out of you and is not something to be grasped for or designed. We know this at the final stage of our spiritual journey, only after we have grappled with the ego's conditioning and can clearly see the truth of who we are.

Dismantling Our Belief Systems

It may shock you to read that *all* your beliefs are false. They are not the ultimate truth. The ultimate truth is experienced universally. That must be the way, or else it can't be the *ultimate truth*.

I would say there is only one ultimate truth: the awareness that "I am."

Put another way, the universal truth is "I am aware." think you would find one person on the planet who would disagree with that statement. That's because it is not a belief. It is a deep experience of one's true nature.

But as soon as I say, "I am this or that," then I start having thoughts and opinions and the ego gets back into play in my mind.

Every belief you hold is the result of an *opinion*, a thought that has crossed your mind with which you agree. Your freedom lies in seeing this.

Personally, I know my opinions about Reiki are only my opinions. Therefore, I hold them lightly and change them regularly—as my tolerant students will tell you!

If you are not questioning and shifting your opinions, your philosophy, and your personal truth periodically, then you may want to consider why not.

In this book, you will notice I may have many opinions, but I never tell you to have them too, I simply invite you to look within, to see if your opinion matches mine. If not, then what is truer for you?

Years ago, I attended Byron Katie's School for the Work. Katie is a master at dismantling belief structures using a simple tool of inquiry, which involves four questions, beginning with the question "Is it true?" Her premise is that no beliefs are true, but if you are going to hold some (and they definitely can be useful for life navigation), then make them pleasant ones. The School focuses on exposing the false belief structure behind stressful thoughts (why change the pleasant ones?!) and is a huge blessing in terms of clearing our conditioning.

During the retreat I attended with Byron Katie, which lasted for nine days, I found many of my beliefs dropping away as I saw repeatedly that every belief around which I had structured my philosophy of life was not true, not true, not true. Towards the end of the retreat, the thought, *Reiki is good. Is it true?* popped into my head. This petrified me, as I realized that this was also going to be seen through. If Reiki was not good, then what about me and my life as a Reiki teacher?

In the end, I saw that Reiki was life force, and as such, neither good nor bad. It is beyond all our concepts and beliefs around it. This realisation gave me immense peace as it stopped any need in me to prove anything to anyone or persuade sceptics. Reiki is my spiritual path, and if anyone wants to join me on it, then wonderful. If not, then that's fine too.

This is the paradox of loosening up the conditioning. It feels counterintuitive because the world seems to expect us to have opinions about everything—questions like: Which political party do you support? What are your religious beliefs? What do you think about current affairs? The fear we have in our minds is that if we have no strong opinions, then our lives are purposeless, and we could become directionless. But the complete opposite is, in fact, true. When we are rigid in our opinions life has a very hard time flowing through us. If we have solidified ego structures that provide little freedom, we will be trapped in our own minds. When we loosen things up and become curious, by contrast, then a delightful explorative joy begins to peek through.

Life is infinitely fascinating and extraordinary, and when you allow this force to shine out of you, then you too experience your life as extraordinary.

A Little Story

Very early in my Reiki career, I worked with an amazing lady who was diagnosed with Stage 4 breast cancer. She experienced amazing success using Reiki, extending a six-month life expectancy to three more years of healthy life. The cancer went into remission, and she was declared cancer-free—for a while. But then the cancer returned.

Towards the end of her life, when it became clear she was dying, I was so devastated by my "failure" as a Reiki practitioner, and so upset by the fact Reiki "had not worked," that I was unable to be present for the woman or her family. I couldn't face my own belief system, so I couldn't face them. During those last few months of her life, I didn't feel comfortable visiting her in hospital or checking in with her family because, to be brutally honest, I was too overwhelmed by my own opinions and thoughts: *Why hasn't Reiki worked? What have I done wrong? What should I have done differently? How can this be happening?*

Despite being in such a close and intense healing relationship with the woman for three years, I couldn't find the resilience or courage to remain strong for her. It was a very painful lesson that still brings remorse to this day.

Ten years later, I worked with another client in very similar circumstances. Her prognosis was dire, and she had also been using Reiki to successfully extend her quality of life for several years. This time, during the final months of life, I was able to be with my client and help her through the pain, disappointment, and fear. It was a totally different experience for me: no less filled with grief, but without guilt, shame, or blame. I was able to be fully present when this second woman most needed it, and I was able to face her fear with her without shying away. We spent many sessions crying together and laughing together, my heart bursting. When she passed away, I was filled with sadness, but I also witnessed her immense courage, spirit, and radiance.

This client still stands out in my mind as one of the most incredible women I have ever met, and I feel humbled and honoured to have been a part of her journey. I was able to be there with a steady and open heart because I no longer held the beliefs and expectations of what Reiki should/shouldn't do and can/can't do.

When you set aside your beliefs and take a closer look, I believe you will see a life filled to the brim with extraordinary moments and experiences as I did.

Coming into Your Own Truth

Let us now journey into your own experience with Reiki and assess which beliefs and conditioning you can let go, and which still serve. Be clear that beliefs are not bad; they are just ultimately not true. Nothing about our egos is bad; they are simply misguided.

Opinions are helpful. Algorithms are helpful. Knowing we prefer tuna pasta to spaghetti Bolognese helps us choose efficiently at a restaurant. Preferences are important life tools that hold our days in some form of order. We are only considering conditioning that stops our freedom and restricts our experience of life as a joyful, creative expression.

In the next chapter, I will ask you to turn your attention to your Reiki education, so you may explore the items in your toolbox. Which Reiki tools serve you, which make you feel restricted? Giving yourself permission to design your own Reiki practice is not only liberating, but also an important step towards self-empowerment. However a note in terms of context, this book focuses on your own spiritual journey, your own self-practice, I am not making any comment on education in terms of professional Reiki practitioner training whereby you are giving treatments to clients or in a medical setting. Obviously in these circumstances your professional education is very important and must follow the guidelines of your training.

A Finger Pointing to the Moon

All words about spiritual values are just hints. Don't hold onto the words as if they are realities. They are hints, almost the way I can point to the moon with my finger—but don't catch hold of my finger. My finger is not the moon.
Look at the moon where the finger is pointing. Forget the finger . . .

—Osho

Reiki is not a philosophy or a belief system. Your Reiki education is designed to help you navigate life and grow. It is a finger pointing to the moon. It is not the actual moon.

Give yourself permission to find your own truth. Your Reiki teacher's philosophy is your teacher's philosophy, yours is yours, and others' is theirs. No truth, no right, no wrong. Take time to experience Reiki free from dogma and come to your own conclusions because, as Osho says in *Zarathustra, A God that Can Dance*, "Only the truth that is your own liberates. Anybody else's truth always becomes a bondage."[1]

Reiki as a practice may have many rules or no rules, many beliefs or none. Your teacher probably teaches differently from me, and the lessons you are taught will be different too. This really doesn't matter so long as you give yourself permission to keep what works and throw out what doesn't. If you are tied to a set of structures that do not serve you, you will never be self-empowered; they will become bondage.

Finding freedom through your Reiki practice includes getting rid of rules and rigid beliefs that do not serve you, and holding true to your own experiences, whether your Reiki teacher likes it or not.

In this chapter, we will explore the more common dos and don'ts of Reiki and push the boundary of what to drop and what to keep. Essentially, anything that makes you feel restricted is good to drop, whereas anything that holds you to a higher ethical standard is best to keep.

Is Your Reiki Practice Self-Empowering?

A guiding principle to help you navigate all kinds of petty rules and regulations on how to apply Reiki in your daily life is how they make you feel. The purpose of your practice is to bring you closer to your inner truth and to encourage self-reflection and inner exploration. Doing so should be something that improves your quality of life.

Over the years, the appeal of Reiki has broadened and the original lineage from Japan to other countries has split into many different branches, each with its own attunement system, nuances, and interpretation of the history and practices of Reiki. I think we can safely say the five precepts of Usui have survived relatively intact, but everything else—from the hand positions in a treatment to the symbols—has undergone all sorts of evolution.

Knowledge of what was original has long been lost to Usui and Usui alone. Arguing about it and calling any lineage the "pure one" is both inaccurate and unhelpful. It's like fighting over fingers and forgetting the moon. As you navigate your education, keep your aim clear—intend to find your own inner truth.

Depending on your lineage, there are many rituals, meditations, breathing techniques, mantras, and methodologies that you may have been taught that you find useful. These techniques are part of your Reiki education. In that respect, they may be useful, although your adherence to them needs to be held lightly.

My lineage is very light on technique. I didn't learn breathing techniques, extra mantras, or really any other technologies apart from the basics of hands-on healing, sending Reiki, and attuning. In a sense, I feel blessed that there was no confusion. I was told, "This is what you do. Now go do it daily." I feel no great urge to learn more techniques. I prefer the stripped-down version I was given by my teacher, as it suits my personal preference for simplicity.

My suggestion, if you feel burdened by tools, is to go back to the basics. Of course, if the tools serve you, then keep them. In all spiritual pathways, there are the more elaborate ritualistic routes as well as stripped-down versions. The problems only begin when people think one way is better than another and try to impose their beliefs on other people.

It is common on any spiritual path to become more fixated on the practice than the outcome; I have seen this in many other modalities, like yoga and meditation, where the focus is on the technique and the perfection of the technique—so that very little spiritual growth happens, even if your headstands are spectacular! The following suggestions focus on shaking up your thoughts around a too-controlled practice.

It is important to focus on the outcome when you do your Reiki. What do you want as the result of your practice? More clarity? More wisdom? More empowerment? Knowing what you want helps enormously when it comes to evaluating if the techniques you employ are helpful.

Reiki Hands-on Self-Treatment

Maybe you were taught eight, twelve, or sixteen hand positions and told to hold each for two, three, or five minutes. Maybe your treatment time is half an hour or an hour. Start with what you have been taught, approaching it with sincerity and discipline. For one month, do your daily practice exactly as instructed and track how you feel. From the base point of direct experience, you can subsequently expand or contract the number of hand positions and stretch out or decrease the time frame to whatever you feel will suit you better.

But you need to start by creating a base point. Then compare.

Remember, the purpose of self-treatment is inner exploration. Can you do Reiki in five minutes while seated in front of the TV and uncover your true nature? Probably not.

Be clear on what it is you want from Reiki. Is it a spiritual pathway for you? Are you willing to explore that path deeply and with serious intent?

In my lineage, we have three treatment protocols at Reiki Level 1: a twelve-hand-position, one-hour treatment; a fifteen-minute chakra-balancing treatment; and an intuitive treatment that encourages students to place their hands wherever they feel drawn to put them, holding them in those locations for as long as they want. I feel this breadth of variation encourages experimentation and gives my students permission to mix and match and follow their intuitions.

Whatever protocols you have been taught, hold them lightly and be willing to extend yourself to find and experiment with other treatment protocols.

Breaking Free of Rules

I have come across a long list of dos and don'ts in researching this book. Regulations can be stifling as they halt creative expression and self-empowerment. People become too afraid to explore their practices genuinely for fear of breaking the rules.

Some examples of rules I am talking about (and my opinions about them) below. They are not described to dismiss the teaching as wrong. Just to point out the opportunity to experiment with the judgment that lives behind the rules and see for yourself. Of course, when Reiki masters teach these rules, they believe a rule to be true—and it is *for them*. But what is my truth is not necessarily your truth, and vice versa. As we have already discussed, there is no ultimate truth regarding any rules we could formulate around Reiki.

Examples of rules that have raised my eyebrows include the following.

- **You are not allowed to drink coffee or alcohol, to eat meat, and so on.** Many Reiki students notice changing food preferences that are natural and effortless when they occur. But Reiki is not a diet. If you feel better when you adhere to a dietary restriction, then you know to follow it. But if you don't feel better, then it is also perfectly OK to do as you please. There is no need to purify yourself or avoid any foods or drinks. Your true self is not found in a food type.
- **You must keep your fingers closed and your hands tight when doing Reiki.** This makes no sense to me! Try it out and do whatever feels best and most relaxing to you. Your hands are simply channelling universal energy, beginning focal points; eventually, you will feel the flow of Reiki throughout your body and your environment.
- **Hand positions need to be done in order.** Reiki connects us with our inner truth. It is an inwards exploration. There is no area that needs to go first, second, or third. Maybe you like to have a routine and ritual. Maybe you like to shake it up a bit. Either way, just go for it! I go through phases with different preferences. It helps to have a routine sometimes. Other times, consistency becomes a limitation.
- **The timing of every hand position needs to be exact.** My understanding is that Usui used no particular hand positions or timings; he just placed his hands onto people until he intuited that he should stop. Who knows, maybe he just stopped when he had another appointment or fancied a

cup of tea! The idea that we need to regulate our spiritual journey via a stopwatch seems nonsensical to me.

- **You are not allowed to Reiki certain areas of the body.** Due to local custom, Reiki is often taught in a way that accommodates certain cultural conventions. For example, in Thailand the crown area is sacred and not to be touched by other people. In some philosophies, the belly button is seen as the centre of the soul and therefore not to be touched. Follow what feels right to you during self-treatment and be respectful of the sensitivities of your clients. Also bear in mind that life force moves through all body parts and be open to exploring yours fully.

- **You are not allowed to Reiki pregnant women.** I used Reiki throughout my two pregnancies and was blessed with little discomfort, nausea, or ill effects. Thank goodness for Reiki, is all I can say! I have no idea who originated this belief, but it is certainly not accurate to my experience.

- **You are not allowed to Reiki for certain illnesses for fear of the sickness getting worse or spreading.** I understand there can be a lot of fear when you are diagnosed with a life-threatening illness and you would have a desire not to rock the boat. You must go with your own feelings around this prescription and respect other peoples' fears if you are offering Reiki to them and they refuse it. I have applied Reiki as a healing modality to people affected by every possible range of illness and have never felt an intuitive whisper that it was making anything worse.

And on and on the list goes. The key thing is to give yourself permission to explore. What happens if you do it differently in your self-treatments? Do you feel better or not? Delve into your inner space and find the wise part of you that is clear and knowing. Trust its guidance.

This wise part is in all of us, no exception.

If something in your practice feels restrictive, give yourself permission to change it—that is the definition of self-empowerment: self-authorisation! Be willing to experiment and explore, and don't take everything your teacher says as gospel. If something works for them, maybe it will work for you too—and maybe not.

When Reiki comes into your life, you find that an entirely new dimension opens—or you intuitively feel that this dimension exists, but you just can't relax into it enough to access it. It's important to realize at this juncture that your spiritual practice is distinct from your education. In this respect, you have total freedom to develop, explore, and deepen your Reiki practice however you need in order to get the most out of it.

Anything that is a judgment is exactly that and should be held lightly. Reiki doesn't judge your style of practise, and you can't do it wrong. Once you put your hands on your body, Reiki flows, and that's it—pure and simple.

In the end, you must figure out the parameters of your practice for yourself. Your body and its needs are individual, and you will likely need to engage in some trial-and-error learning to understand these needs fully. Most importantly, it's a good idea to get in the habit of listening to your body and investing time and honest effort to hear its messages to you with clarity. This is what it takes to establish a great ongoing relationship with your body.

If we listen to the body, we always can feel confident that we know where to place our hands, how long to do it for, and whether a morning, evening, or a lunchtime treatment suits us best. All this kind of information is there for us, if we are willing to inquire.

If you have been trained in a style of Reiki practice with many rules, what should you be doing to lessen the burden of them or to see if they will continue to be your truth going forward? Two keys can help you blend your Reiki education with your spiritual practice.

- Respect everything you've been taught, and hold it lightly
- Remember that rules should hold you to a higher integrity

Respect Everything You're Been Taught, and Hold It Lightly

Question everything. Does it work for you? Does it feel tight and restrictive? Does it feel empowering and supportive? Does it feel expansive? It requires a level of sincerity and dedication to not just take what your teacher has said is right, but to hold it up against your own experience.

As I said previously, if you choose to do things differently than you were taught, make sure you have a base measure against which to compare your results. For example: If your teacher instructed you to use a strict sequence of hand positions, then do the sequence regularly for a few months so you can see the effect it is having on you. After that, if you feel you want to loosen up the system, then, by all means, experiment to see if this improves things or at the very least makes no difference. If things feel less aligned, then go back to the original sequence or move on to other variations until you come to an approach that feels right to you.

Your teacher is passing on knowledge on the way he or she was taught or sees things. Respect that your teacher has been doing Reiki a lot longer than you have and may have run several experiments of his or her own that garnered results you would find valuable. Do not be conned by your ego. Be certain to measure your experiments against an inner bullshit monitor.

On occasions when my students inform me that the one-hour treatment doesn't work for them—so they are opting for the fifteen-minute chakra balancing treatment instead—I quiz them as to how many times they tried the one-hour treatment. Then I usually get some vague reply, like, "Oh, a couple of times."

Challenge yourself to twenty-one days of full one-hour Reiki self-treatments. See for yourself. The response is always very positive and surprising for people who have never done a dedicated Reiki one-hour self-treatment previously. Rarely do I get the feedback that it doesn't work for someone. Set your bullshit monitor to perceive twenty-one days of continuous practice as a bare minimum for testing out any new changes in th[e] practice Reiki.

Rules Should Hold You to a Higher Integrity

The five precepts of Usui are a good mindset to embrace for maintaining integrity with your personal practice. These have various translations, and the version I resonate with was given to me in my Reiki 1 class:

> *Just for today, I will not anger.*
> *Just for today, I will not worry.*
> *Just for today, I will have an attitude of gratitude.*
> *Just for today, I will do my inner work honestly.*
> *Just for today, I will show kindness.*[1]

These precepts are designed to give us orientation in how we approach ourselves and those we treat. They hold us to higher integrity when the ego gets on its high horse.

The one thing you can be sure of when you begin to get somewhere in your spiritual journey is that the ego will be right there beside you, trying to use your growth for its own aggrandisement. Every insight will be an opportunity for it to preach to you. Every release will be an opportunity to tell you you've healed. These precepts will help you be steady. Just ask, are you living the precepts? Or is there still work to be done?

It is often very telling to send Reiki to precepts you think you have nailed, just to see what happens. My students tell me they are frequently shocked to learn how far they are from where they thought. For example, a usually calm and collected person could fly into a rage after sending Reiki to "I will not anger." Someone who thinks he is full of gratitude will be snappy and rude or resentful after sending Reiki to "I will have the attitude of gratitude."

I often contemplate the precepts, and I am aware when I am acting out of accordance with them, but I have also found them not so helpful when I use them as a stick to beat myself. When I do get angry, I am more curious as to what triggered the anger and less concerned about the breaking of the precept. This is what I mean by *holding the rules lightly.*

Rules that make you ponder deeper spiritual questions are helpful. For example, pondering the five precepts of Usui may be helpful. But worrying about whether you did thirty-six minutes of Reiki or only thirty-four minutes—not so.

Rules that make you feel restricted or stressed should be looked at carefully to discern if it has merit. Worrying about your clothing, your diet, and your hand positions simply adds to your stress and is the opposite of what we are trying to achieve with our Reiki practices. Part of coming into your own inner wisdom is to embrace your choices and be willing to make a choice because it feels right to you, not because your teacher said so.

Reiki is universal life force. I cannot tell you how profound a gift it is that we can readily access it and go with its flow. Lifeforce is what moves the cosmos, creates everything, and supports all manifested beings and things. Do you really think the way we practice has to be done in an uptight, restrictive, fearful way? It makes no sense given the diversity of the universe! Open to the energy, expand with it, journey deeply, and let it work you—stop trying to work it. You'll experience much deeper joy and much greater self-empowerment if you do.

Along the way, be respectful of what you have been taught. There is great wisdom in what is handed down, so hold it all and then observe what serves you and what doesn't. Give yourself permission to drop restrictive practices. But be mindful that dropping practices or recommendations simply because you don't want to dedicate yourself to your inner work is not spiritual wisdom. You may just be acting lazy.

At the end of the day, you are only cheating yourself if you act lazy or resistant. Nobody else. Keep your integrity and find the correct balance of freedom in your Reiki practice and courage to dedicate yourself to finding your truth.

3.
Understanding the Reiki Symbols

It is the external, or lower, expression
of the higher truth which is symbolized,
and is a means of communicating
realities which might otherwise be either
obscured by the limitations of language or
too complex for adequate expression.

—J.C. Cooper

At Reiki Level 2, we are introduced to three Reiki symbols: Power, Harmony, and Connection.* During my Reiki 2 class, I was immediately captivated by what I learned. It was like an internal light bulb clicked on, and I knew I had stepped into something very significant. I was working in advertising at the time, so knew first-hand the power of symbology. Even so, working with Reiki symbols was a totally different experience and brought a level of sacred awe to my spiritual practice that had hitherto been absent.

* To preserve the integrity of the symbols, they will be referred to by their resonance rather than by their Japanese names.

The emphasis on the Reiki symbols varies enormously in the teaching and practice of Reiki. Many Reiki teachers only use the symbols sporadically or during attunements or when sending energy to others, which I find surprising. The Reiki symbols are keys that open doors we encounter along the spiritual path, and I hope this chapter inspires you to deepen your relationship with them.

Understanding Symbology

The Reiki 2 attunement essentially invites you into the world of the Reiki symbols. If we look at symbology as nothing more than logos it may help the more sceptical amongst us come to logical terms with what is happening. Logos are humanmade symbols, and their power to convey branding, image, messaging, values, and recognition is beyond dispute. Companies spend billions on logo design and ongoing brand recognition. Colours, shapes, and the psychology behind logos are well researched before they are utilized by advertising agencies. Constant and consistent messaging builds images, values, and feelings that consumers can describe in detail when asked what they think a brand stands for by researchers.

They can tell simply by being shown a well-known logo.

Logos are simple energy symbols, with information built through advertising dollars and consistent messaging. Any symbol, when engaged with energetically, builds information. Some symbols have been around for many generations and have well established and frequent inputs of energy—think of the many common religious symbols you know, such as the Christian cross or the Hindu Om. Billions of people over thousands of years have contributed to the sacred functioning of such symbols, whose meaning has a profound effect on users. When we evoke sacred symbols, we evoke the power, energy, and information that has been embedded into their energy field by all those who used them before us.

Biologist Rupert Sheldrake calls this phenomenon of building a field of energy *morphic resonance*.[1] He has researched extensively a variety of situations that lend credibility to his hypothesis. In one experiment, he taught English schoolchildren Japanese rhymes. One was a very famous Japanese nursery rhyme that had been sung by millions of Japanese over many years. The other rhyme was a jumble of Japanese words and sounds that had the same rhyme scheme and metre. The English children learned the well-known rhyme significantly more quickly than the nonsensical one, despite both rhymes being in a foreign language.[2] Sheldrake postulates that *morphic resonance* associated with all previous recitations of the nursery rhyme allowed the information to be much more easily accessed and known. Essentially, he says, the English children had access to an energy field, a *morphic field*, built by millions of Japanese children before them and this made it easier for them to learn it.

The idea of a morphic field around all things, which is enhanced and built upon over time, is a fascinating idea and it may be the reason why so many rituals in our lives, such as blowing out candles on our birthdays or celebrating Christmas even if we are not religious, hold such strong significance for many of us.

Morphic resonance, the theory that *all similar things resonate with past similar things*, is a concept that helps to explain not only the power of the symbols but also the power of the Reiki attunement process. The fields of information help to give us access to areas of power and support that we cannot usually access on our own.

Psychologist Carl Jung viewed the aspect of human behaviour, including instinctual fears and tendencies, as a result of evolutionary ancestral memory, from shared human history, the *collective unconscious*. He used the idea of the collective unconscious to explain why similar dreams, literature, symbology, art, and religious thought appears in different cultures.

Whether or not you agree with these theories of why symbols enable us to access deeper areas of information, as someone that uses Reiki symbols you can determine the impact that they have on you during your Reiki self-treatments for yourself. Most of my Reiki students report that their treatments feel stronger when they incorporate the symbols. It is also my experience that most family members notice an increase in the intensity of the Reiki in the hands of a student who has completed Level 2 as compared to Level 1.

As a Reiki student, you can carry out simple experiments for yourself to self-treat with or without symbols to see what you think.

My belief is that these symbols contain energetic information that has been amplified by millions of Reiki students using, activating, and building upon the original information intended by Mikao Usui. It is my experience that the symbols have grown more powerful over the twenty years I have been using them.

The concept of the symbols having their own information energy fields, and that these fields are evolving and growing as the practice of Reiki expands, is the theory with which I work in this book. Seeing Reiki symbols as having morphic fields helps us to see them as sacred. When activating them for our own use, I would hope we do so with mindful intention and respect, impressed by the knowledge that we are part of the symbols' purity of meaning. Our usage of the symbols either strengthens their focus and meaning or dilutes them, depending on how we employ the symbols and with what intention.

In my opinion (and I realize it is not universally held), as part of the invitation to access and utilize the sacred power of the symbols, we become guardians of their integrity. This is a sacred invitation and one we shouldn't take lightly.

With this philosophy in mind, I will not be using the names of the symbols in this book but will refer to them via their innate symbolic resonance: Power, Harmony, Connection, and Master.

The Symbol Advantage

When you step into the symbols' robust morphic fields, their resonance can magnify your similar intention and focus. In this way, you are supported by symbols. Their resonance gives you more access to the information in each field than working on your own with an intention. But *how* is this happening? There are two different ways of looking at this. From a *relative* (me and the symbols) stance, the symbols are helping me do something "extra."

For example, sometimes I walk into a room and I get an uneasy feeling. My skin will get goose bumps or "prickles." I interpret this as a sign of the environment not being in harmony. To help balance the atmosphere in the room, I will invoke the Harmony symbol and nine times out of ten the room feels better immediately (or at least my skin stops crawling around). It would appear the symbol has helped me in my intention to banish any energy that was causing my discomfort.

The second way of looking at this example is from an *absolute* perspective: I and the symbol are in fact the same source. If you pay attention when you visualise the symbols in the room, you will notice that your body has a reaction too. For me, the sensation is in my heart centre and radiates outwards into my entire chest cavity; and if I continue to invoke Harmony, the buzzing sensations continue to radiate, getting stronger throughout my body.

The Harmony symbol could well be resonating with the harmony in my body and in the room. In this sense, I, the symbol, and the room all resonate with harmony because of my intention to balance everything. I am using the symbol as a tool to bring attention to the harmony already present.

Exploring this aspect of what is really being affected when you use your Reiki symbols is an important aspect of coming into your own understanding of these tools and will most likely change as you shift your perspective from the relative to the absolute.

It is also important to explore the theory that the symbols have power beyond what you yourself can intend, otherwise what would be their purpose apart from useful reminders?

There are some Reiki lineages that do not use symbols. They may have originally derived from Usui, or from someone completely different—I am unsure. But coming across one such lineage during a holistic festival, I was curious to try a session. I sat down and the practitioner placed her hands above my head. I could feel an immediate warmth and glow through my head and down into my body and it felt wonderful. As the session progressed, I could feel myself deepening and dropping into a lovely meditation.

This is a well-trodden path for me, as I often go to very deep, quiet spaces when I do self-treatments with Reiki, so not only was this depth familiar, but I also knew how deep I could go. But we suddenly stopped and hovered at around a 70-per cent depth of where I know I can go on my own. It was a strange sensation to "stop" there. I wanted to drop deeper, but I felt this lady had reached her maximum capacity. It was also curious as I had never experienced this stopping effect when I had Reiki treatments using symbols.

I interpreted this treatment as a first-hand experience of the impact of the symbols—or rather, *of their absence.*

Reiki symbols allow us to go deeper than we can go on our own—the morphic fields of the symbols are bigger and more potent than our individual energy fields, and so both we and those we treat step into these fields and deepen when the symbols invoke the resonance of their fields.

But don't just believe me when I say this. Please experiment for yourself! Swap a treatment with a Reiki friend and do half an hour with no symbols, then do half an hour with symbols. Measure the impact for yourself.

Reiki symbols are invaluable tools for personal growth, each symbol has its own morphic field and "personality" and understanding them will help you to harness their field of information. Let's look now at further understanding the information in the symbols for Power, Harmony, and Connection.

The Power Symbol

In my experience, the symbols amplify certain abilities within our own systems. The Power symbol helps us to focus, empower, and strengthen. It has a masculine, or yang, signature. Visualising the Power symbol over our hands when we give ourselves or others Reiki gives the Reiki flow a boost—I liken this to the effect of putting your thumb over a hose when the water is running: The water shoots out more powerfully.

The Power symbol can be very helpful in shifting stubborn energy blocks or resistance. It also helps us intensify our Reiki giving above and beyond the power we could achieve exclusively with our own intention, as a little personal experimentation will show you.

If you are not already using the Power symbol in your self-treatments, simply begin incorporating a few visualisations of it over your hands every time you change your hand position.

To experiment with the activation of the symbol, visualise the symbol directly over the palm of your hand and use the spiral to focus the Reiki through your hands and into your body.

Another fun thing to try to deepen your connection to the Power symbol is drawing it directly on the soles of your feet for grounding. It has the effect of activating the minor chakras in your feet to bring more awareness into your lower chakras. This is especially useful if you are feeling flighty or too mentally active.

The feeling of not being grounded commonly arises when we do too much in our heads. That can include too much meditation (yes, that really is a thing!), too much computer work, and too much chatting on social networks. The feeling of being ungrounded is a bit like being out of your body and disconnected. Physical symptoms may include dizziness, clumsiness, lacking direction or focus, and frequent daydreaming. Ungroundedness makes it difficult to achieve things, like meeting deadlines or getting through our to-do lists. But more than this, it means that we are not present and available for those around us.

Empowering the energy field of anything with the Power symbol can be fun, too. This includes empowering your food, water, personal spaces, crystals—anything really! Taking time to experiment with this symbol and feeling the effects of it as stand-alone energy will be invaluable to you in deepening your experience and understanding of Reiki as you move through the stages of spiritual development.

Meditating on the Power symbol is a great way of feeling its effects directly. Simply sitting and imagining the symbol spiralling from your crown through your body and doing this at an easy pace for five minutes will give you a direct experience of what it can do for you. You will also see what I mean when I say each symbol carries information and a certain intention, but it is not personal. The Power symbol strengthens and enhances, so if you find yourself in an angry mood, the Power symbol could make your mood worse!

And more helpfully, if you are already dropping into a deep meditative space, the Power symbol will take you deeper. Don't be afraid to experiment though, I find this amusing to see in action, but on a deeper level it strengthens my respect for the symbols so that I am more mindful when using them on others. There is a time to make things more powerful and active, and there is a time to be more receptive and gentler.

The Harmony Symbol

This is my personal favourite symbol, as I am always desiring a little more balance within myself or with other people and my environment. If the Power symbol represents masculine yang energy, the Harmony symbol represents the compassionate feminine yin energy. The Harmony symbol carries the morphic resonance of balance, concordance, synchronicity, and agreement.

Some Reiki practitioners say the Power symbol connects us with our lower chakras and the Harmony symbol connects us with our upper chakras. Personally, I see these two symbols as associated with the complementary forces of action and reception. When we visualize harmony in a specific place or person (like ourselves during our self-treatments), it is beneficial to follow it up with the Power symbol to empower our intention to harmonise. The Power symbol can be used to empower the Harmony symbol itself. To add some *oomph* to it, if you like.

There is a long list of uses for Harmony, bringing more balance and clarity to spaces and environments, people and objects, crystals, and water. For the purpose of the spiritual path, I would like you to use Harmony on yourself more. Try to remember this tool when you are feeling upset, angry, irritated, or frustrated. Imagine the symbol in front of you, activate the space it opens, and then step into it.

Another lovely way to activate harmony within you is to imagine the symbol on top of your crown, and then slowly sink the symbol down through all your chakras and out your feet. If your visualisation skills are not so good, then actually finger-draw the symbol in front of you and step into the space, taking the time to really notice any impact it has on you.

The more you experiment and see the effects of the Harmony symbol for yourself, the more likely you are to really connect and form a close alliance with the information contained within it. Explore where you feel the symbol resonating in your body, is it in the heart centre? Or somewhere else? Experiment with it, activate it, and really come into your own personal relationship with this amazing symbol.

As with the Power symbol, meditating with Harmony is the best way to have a direct experience of its effects. The good news is that even if you are in an angry mood this symbol will help to calm you down. Often, if I find I am distracted, moody, or busy with cyclical thoughts, I begin my meditation with several rounds of visualising the Harmony symbol coming down through the crown of my head and into my body, and once I am feeling calmer I then switch to the Power symbol to deepen the meditation.

There seems to be an ongoing debate about if it is ethical to visualize the different symbols on others without their permission, and I agree that it is a tricky decision. My general guideline is always to ask permission if you are using Reiki on someone as this has the potential to make very real shifts in the person's energy field. No matter how good your intention, what seems right for you may not be right for the other, and vice versa. I am sure you would want to know if someone was messing with your energy.

However, in terms of showering someone with the Harmony symbol, I feel that this is something that can be done if that person is obviously out of balance. It is more like asking someone to reset or take a breath—we are not adding anything extra, giving any extra energy, or messing with his or her energy in any way when we use it. The Harmony symbol simply opens and holds space for a readjustment to occur should someone want to make one.

What are ways to see this effect in action? Visualize the Harmony symbol over rooms, spaces, and people who feel out of balance. I enjoy doing this when I'm idle, such as when I'm waiting to check out at the grocery store, in a traffic jam, or walking my dog. I visualize Harmony over irate customers, impatient queues, and tantrumming infants, sometimes with delightful results. People calm down, babies stop crying, environments lighten up. It can be amazing, really. The trick, as always, is to hold the results lightly—don't be attached. Sometimes it works, sometimes it doesn't.

You are not carrying out any empirical testing here. And you are not manipulating anyone. You are holding a harmonising space and people may heed the invitation and take the opportunity to calm down and relax—but not always. As you know in your own experience, we can carry ill feelings long after events have passed. We can easily hang on to frustration or impatience, even when the energy is lovely and calm. The Harmony symbol is simply an invitation. That's why it can be done without asking permission.

The Connection (Sending) Symbol

The Connection symbol is thought to be made up of several overlapping *kanji*, Japanese words. The most likely representation of it is made up of five words, which together mean "I am pure thought." Note that this is a very loose translation, as the kanji for *I* can also mean *one* (as in all of us), and the kanji for *thought* is made up of two words, which separately mean *heart* and *mind*.

The beauty of the Japanese language is its varied nuances and double meanings. Essentially the entire language is built on symbology! That which makes it profound, also makes it problematic when trying to relay the meaning in English. What I feel Usui was trying to convey with the Connection symbol is the idea that we are all connected, as in "one/all is heart/mind," and the idea that with correct intention we can create action, as in "I am pure thought." This message is profound and encapsulates both the relative and absolute viewpoint.

The Connection symbol gives us the ability to send Reiki to any morphic field—including thoughts, situations, and intentions—which gives us an amazing tool to gain insights. Sending Reiki to people is a wonderful addition to our Reiki toolkit, but the real power of Reiki as a spiritual path comes through our ability to use the Connection symbol to connect with ourselves. As we work with this symbol's morphic resonance we see the dual truth of "I am pure thought" *and* "all is heart/mind."

My assumption is that you have already been trained on how to do a basic send using the three symbols we've previously discussed—the Power, Harmony, and Connection symbols. If so, you should follow your lineage techniques, as I have come across many diverse protocols for sending and I do not want to introduce confusion unnecessarily.

If you have not been taught to send to specific thoughts, situations, or intentions, the technique is simple. Just write down something you want to send healing to, and then send Reiki using your lineage technique. There is no specific ritual around this written text; it is just a statement of intent. We shall discuss the process in more detail in Chapter 7, "Deconditioning the Mind." For now, I ask you to hold the idea that the Connection symbol is the key for bringing these two seemingly opposing statements "I am pure thought" and "all is heart/mind" together.

4.
Reiki Attunements for Personal Growth

During the Reiju the student will have an initial experience of the True Self. . . . This initial experience is like a seed . . . rediscovered by the student deep within herself.

—Frans Stiene

The attunement process is what makes Reiki unique from other complementary healing modalities, though tellingly, it also makes it more like many forms of religion. This is because the attunement is an initiation to the Reiki path. It can unnerve people to hear this! It's important for us all to understand that Reiki is not a religion, and it does not have any beliefs or rules attached to it. Even Usui's five precepts are guidelines, not beliefs to be followed.

The reason I feel Reiki is more aligned with religion than most complementary therapies is that it is a pathway to salvation. Like all religions at their root, it is a guidance system to freedom and happiness. But you don't have to wait until death to get there! Reiki is a personal spiritual pathway (as we shall discuss in the next chapter), and the attunement is a very important component as it illuminates the path.

The Master Symbol

In my lineage, we split the master level training into Level 3, where the Master symbol is taught along with the heart attunement (*reiju*), and the Teacher level, where the remainder of the attunements are taught, plus months of study to become a competent Reiki master teacher. There is a shift in students, first as they step into the Master symbol energy, and second, as they begin to embody Reiki more and more through teaching and passing on Reiki to others.

The Master symbol is a kanji derivative meaning "big bright light." I love this idea that at the end of it all, we are just big, bright lights. It is also derived from the Buddhist idea of an *enlightened nature*.

I call the Master symbol the symbol of transformation, and I do not take this description lightly. In fact, during my Level 3 class, I promise students they will not recognize themselves a year later, assuming they are assiduously practising the techniques, doing attunements, and engaged in their inner work. And I have yet to be proven wrong. The Master symbol is an invitation to transform.

Giving an attunement to another person and bringing them into alignment with Reiki energy is so profound that even after giving thousands of attunements it still leaves me amazed every time. One minute my students have "normal" hands and the next minute there is Reiki blasting out of them. I have no idea how that happens, only that I have participated earnestly in a ritual that was taught to me by my Reiki Master and it works every single time. It's totally bonkers, really.

Explaining attunements is a challenging task. Previously, we discussed the morphic fields of symbols. The Master symbol holds the key to the door of universal life force itself. This is the big, bright light encompassing, in its totality, the energy of the entire light spectrum, and all other frequencies.

During the attunement process a Reiki Master steps into the morphic field of Reiki itself and intends it to flow out of the student's hands. We can direct the energy to come out of any minor chakra, including the chakras in the feet, the eyes, or any of the other points. Usui used to conduct healing using his eyes. Personally, I have had my feet attuned, which is very useful in the winter months!

The flow of Reiki through the hands is a directed intention by a Reiki teacher whose purpose is to help us manage the flow and direct healing more effectively, but it is by no means the only way we can flow with Reiki or have Reiki flow through us.

The Importance of Lineage

During the attunement process, the Reiki master is taught a ritual to follow. This ritual is important as it holds the teacher in a lineage. The ritual itself is a morphic field, a doorway if you like. Every time the ritual is performed in combination with the Reiki symbols, it brings you into the lineage that flows back to Mikao Usui.

As someone aware of his true nature, Usui created his form of Reiki to light the way for others, pointing a finger to the moon, as it were. And the moon, the thing he is pointing to, is the truth that we are all universal source appearing as individuals.

As we step into the attunement process, there is a sense of merging of the attuner, the attuned, and Reiki. This insight changes both the attuner and the attuned. The transformation may be so subtle it seems imperceptible. You may not have felt a thing. But receiving an attunement shifts your personal perception.

As a Reiki master following the ritual, you yourself do not have to be enlightened and aware of your true nature (thank goodness!), because Usui carved out the path for you those many decades ago. All you need to do is use the symbols and the attunement ritual, as it was taught to you. Think of it like you would a piece of music. The enlightened master was the composer who wrote the symphony, and you only have to follow the musical score to recreate the master's genius. You do not have to know how to write beautiful music in order to play it, but you do have to practice playing your "instrument" if you want to follow the score accurately. And you must be able to intuit the sacred beauty of the "notes" you are playing.

This is the gift of the attunement process. It is a sacred doorway, but the opening of the door can be learned by anyone, there is no great spiritual attainment required, just dedication to practice the process and open the door wide. It is also true that anyone can walk through the doorway, anyone can be attuned to Reiki because we all resonate with universal source, that is our original nature.

As you merge with universal source, you recognize the truth of your inner essence, even if it doesn't enter your conscious thought. You could argue that we already are universal source so why do we even need an attunement? And yes, we are, but much like how symbols work on an absolute level, you could also say we are already in harmony, and empowered, and connected, but these are only concepts and not helpful if they do not feel true for you. If you have not *recognised* that you are all those things, and if you have not recognised that you are source manifested as a person, then the symbols and attunements are tools of use to you.

Effectively the Reiki master uses the attunement ritual to step into universal life force setting up a resonance—to use a very loose analogy imagine all the cells begin to vibrate with universal source. The *attunee* (the one being attuned to Reiki) also begins to resonate, as we are all essentially universal source. In that moment, recognition is created in the attunee that he or she is Reiki too. Something deep in them sparks, or as Frans Stiene puts it, a seed is rediscovered. Nothing is being added to the person receiving an attunement, the Reiki master is not passing anything on or channelling anything, it is more akin to sound resonance, when I vibrate at a certain frequency and then you recognise this and the part of you that recognises it begins to vibrate too. For many people, it is an instant recognition that ignites the hands and creates physical sensations, such as heat, tingling, cold, or prickling in the hands or the body, or visual cues, such as colours or flashes of lights when the eyes are closed. For others, it takes some time and practice to become sensitive to the new flow in us.

I am aware that not all lineages will agree with my description, and in some Reiki classes they state that the students must practice for a period before the Reiki will flow. I have not extensively researched the differences in attunements or expectations so I can only describe my own lineage's process and for us the attunement process produces an immediate and tangible flow of Reiki that most students feel during the Level 1 workshop itself, no practice or experience required. It may be due to the morphic field and expectation of my lineage; and for sure, it would be interesting to further research this aspect of Reiki. It is useful to note that not all attunements are the same and yet all the different doors still open to Reiki.

Attuning to Universal Flow

The reiju (Heart attunement) is the final tool in your Reiki toolbox. If you are a Level 3/Reiki master who has not been taught how to self-attune, the instructions are simple. Set up to do your Heart attunement as you would for another person, placing your photo on the chair where the attunee would customarily be seated. Do the attunement around your photo imagining yourself sitting there, exactly as if you were another person. Do it mindfully, like a sacred meditation.

If you do not have a Heart attunement methodology to follow, then consider ways to experiment with your attunement processes. For example, if you have four of the same ones, then simply do one of them. If you have a series of four for Level 1, then chose the first one. If you have no idea what I am talking about, then seek out a teacher who offers reiju. I offer regular free attunements online via my website, www.Reiki-Centre.com. Use your intuition when choosing a teacher, make sure you resonate with the teacher and feel comfortable with what they are offering.

The point of self-attunements, attuning others, and receiving attunements from a Reiki master is to merge (frequently if possible) with Reiki, the universal source energy. As you relax and become alert to the attunement process, you begin to feel what I am talking about—maybe you resonate with this because you feel your heart chakra expand during every attunement, or maybe you have experienced a sensation of merging where body and air become one. Perhaps there is an intensification of your cellular awareness, like all your cells are buzzing. No matter how it appears to you, see it as an invitation to get acquainted.

For me, an attunement processes through my body as an intense popping sensation in my heart chakra, like a mini explosion in my chest. Frankly, it can be rather intense and not particularly pleasant, but neither is it unpleasant. It's just an experience.

The sensations created by long periods of meditation or intense spiritual practice are like those of Reiki attunements. During a long meditation retreat (not Reiki focused), I began to have these sensations for longer and longer durations. It didn't frighten me, as I knew what it was: I was immersed in universal life force. But for many participants on the retreat who were not as practiced in coming into contact with this intensity, the sensation threw up fear, anxiety, and health concerns. It does sometimes feel like your cells will explode from the intensity, so I understand the fear, and I am grateful that I was introduced to it gradually and over time, through the attunement process.

The experience of merging with source is also useful as it shows you that it is not some kind of blissful existential state. We are grounded, we are awake, we are present in the room and doing what we are doing, and at the same time we feel timeless, formless, and (for many of us) like all kinds of cellular popping and buzzing is going on. It may feel peaceful and it may feel blissful, but it often also feels very ordinary and normal. This familiarity is useful.

Blurbs about enlightenment that we read on spiritual websites or hear repeated in spiritual circles can make us think of spiritual awareness as something different or extraordinary, when really it is more simply shifts of perspective.

Is this merging possible for Reiki practitioners who are not at Level 3/Master or individuals who are not getting attunements? Yes, of course. You can immerse yourself during your Reiki practice of self-treatment. Sending also offers an opportunity to enter this doorway. Granted, attunements are very helpful tools, but when you are dedicated and sincere in your self-treatment, you can feel the same sense of merging, the same sense of expansion, the same feeling of eternity.

As we move next into a discussion of spirituality itself, bear in mind that the self-treatment, the symbols, and the attunements are simply tools, fingers pointing at the moon. It is for you to discover which tools are helpful and which tools to do away with or replace with others. Remember that Usui enlightened without Reiki, he then gave us Reiki and its tools as a gift to help us. The path I describe in Part 2 is not Usui's path; it is mine. But the path I tread would not be possible without the Reiki tools. I also share this path because I have noticed distinct similarities in my journey and the hundreds of others who follow along beside me in my Reiki community. It would seem there is morphic resonance amongst those of us travelling the Reiki spiritual path.

5.
Reiki as a Spiritual Practice

It is important to start from a place close to you, don't start from something distant such as philosophy or logic. . . . Work on your heart and do things from the quiet space inside of you. Anyone can access Reiki, because it begins within yourself!

—Memorial to Mikao Usui at
Saihoji Temple, Tokyo

In 1992, my first introduction to the world of Reiki was simple. Hawayo Takata's lineage was the only one available outside of Japan, and most teachers taught her story and philosophy. I was blessed to find a Reiki teacher, John Veltheim, who had trained with several different Takata-trained Reiki masters. He had already undergone extensive training in martial arts, different schools of meditation, Chinese medicine, including acupuncture, and had a thriving chiropractic clinic in Australia. He was an avid student of energy healing, natural therapies, comparative religion, and philosophy. In my eyes, he was a walking, talking encyclopaedia, as well as intuitive and charismatic. In John's own words, his central philosophy was a "deep-seated conviction that ultimately people should be able to help themselves and maintain their own health."[1] He was attracted to Reiki because, despite all his expertise and years in the healing arts, he had not found an effective system that he could use to treat himself or pass on to his clients which transcended rigid lifestyles or personal motivation. In other words, he found that his clients could not maintain the diets, exercise, and meditation programs necessary to maintain their wellbeing. Like many of us, when he attended his Level 1 class, he felt an inner peace and harmony envelop him that signalled to him he had found what he was looking for.

When I attended John's Level 1 class, I was a complete newbie to natural therapies, energy healing, and eastern religion. John taught from so much experience and wisdom that it never occurred to me that Reiki could or would be taught any other way. He imparted such passion and purpose with his lectures, as well as decades-worth of study, healing experience, and knowledge.

He believed that a Reiki master's job was to teach others Reiki so they could heal themselves. I imagine after so many years as a practitioner trying to heal others, he was delighted to find a way to teach others to "fish for themselves." (The proverb "Give a man a fish, and you feed him for a day. Teach a man to fish, and you feed him for a lifetime" was a favourite of his!) In many ways, John's personal experience influenced my own journey as I resonated with his message: "Reiki is about choices. As an initiate, the extent of your shift in consciousness will be determined according to your level of commitment toward yourself."[2]

When he told me "Self-treating in Reiki is a pathway that could carry someone to a state of enlightenment" I took it seriously and began my own lifelong journey of spiritual discovery.[3] At the time, I had little idea of what enlightenment was, or even what a spiritual path was, but I intuited Reiki was transformational and that the transformative aspect had to come from me.

Today, it seems to me, much effort is being invested in getting Reiki into the health care system and having it be acknowledged as a complementary therapy. The focus of many national Reiki associations is on the regulation and certification of Reiki healthcare practitioners. But are we not missing the point? Reiki is foremost a spiritual practice intended to raise self-awareness. Is it accurate, or wise, to battle the medical profession with a personal growth tool? It seems to me that we are barking up the wrong tree.

Reiki is neither medicine, nor science. Reiki is deep introspection, connection with our truth, developing our inner wisdom. It belongs to meditation, spiritual practices, and yoga. All these practices have abilities to heal, but that is not the primary point of any of them. Meditation is now well researched for its wonderful health and wellbeing benefits, but the point of meditation is not to reduce your blood pressure, that is merely a side effect of a deep and effective practice.[4]

In an interview Usui gave regarding Usui Reiki Ryoho (the name he himself used for Reiki), he said:

> Usui Reiki Ryoho does not only heal physical illness. Mental illnesses, such as agony, weakness, timidity, irresolution, nervousness, and other bad habits, can be corrected. Then you can lead a happy life and heal others with the mind of God or Buddha. That becomes your principal object.[5]

What Usui hints at but may not have been at liberty to openly teach is that Reiki is a path to inner truth. With his phrase the *mind of God*, I suspect he meant the free unconditioned mind.

It is a significant point. Although he taught Reiki as a healing system, his true objective was to help people wake up to the truth within themselves.

I believe Reiki is a spiritual practice disguised as a healing modality.

What Is a Spiritual Practice?

I agree with Deepak Chopra when he tweets: *"Religion is belief in someone else's experience. Spirituality is having your own experience."*[6] Being spiritual is not the same thing as being religious, although it doesn't reject religion. As a spiritual person, you can have a deep experience that indicates for you that Christianity is true for you—or Buddhism, or Hinduism. Spirituality is coming into your own truth and living your life based on that, as opposed to doing what everyone else wants you to do. You can be equally spiritual as a religious or a secular person—what defines a spiritual practice is having a desire to find out who *you* are.

The root of the human spirit—our *animating principle*—should be the focus of our spiritual investigation. A spiritual practice therefore is a very personal definition. Your spiritual practice is the tool or technique you utilise to spend time investigating who you are. It could be a daily meditation routine, yoga practice, jogging, walking in the woods, cooking the evening meal—a time for inner reflection. What I am presenting in this book is a spiritual path that is more detailed than simply reflecting. A path has more guidance and can take us on a deep inner journey based on hints from people who have trodden the path before.

Usui gave us the path of Reiki, leaving us tools to aid us. These tools are for us to engage with personally, in our own ways as contemporary people. The tools do not require us to remain stuck in attitudes of the 1920s or to believe that Reiki practice has not evolved.

In Usui's time, there were already thousands of Reiki students. But now there are millions. Reiki is evolving, it is a helpful, fluid pathway. Humanity is evolving and the speed at which we can integrate is speeding up. The 1920's speed and the 2020's speed of information dissemination is incomparable, so within the Reiki spiritual practice there is always room for evolution.

Authentic spiritual practice has no rules or beliefs. No structures whatsoever. It is just you, figuring yourself out. You may or may not find that you gravitate towards certain methods of spiritual practice, including Reiki. But you will notice that you are on the right spiritual path because your practice feels "right," there is a certain ease to it.

One of my students described this distinction accurately when she was relaying to me her pure joy and relief at finding Reiki. After twenty-five years of arduous and disciplined meditation practice that she felt was almost a daily torture, she could now relax into her Reiki practice as the most natural and effortless expression of her spiritual self. That's the truth of it. When you are on the right spiritual path, you know it because it brings you peace and a sense of rightness that all other methodologies don't.

Many people share a very harmful belief that "life is hard." But is this true? There is lots of gain with less pain if you are truly following the path that is appropriate for you.

When you come into flow with your spiritual practice, it feels like ease and grace. The common belief is that the road to ease and flow is hard, and that the ease is the reward at the end of the hardship. But no! Ease can be there right from the beginning. If your Reiki practice feels hard, make it easier! If what you have been taught is based on the fashion of 1920, update it! Investigating who you truly are is a joyful, exciting uncovering process, not a rigid, painful struggle.

Watch children and their effortless playful exuberance for life. Why do we lose this when we become adults? Is it because we go on a tough spiritual quest or is it because we have strayed from our inner truth and stopped trusting our inner wisdom?

Once we have lost sight of our truth under the layers of our conditioning then yes, life truly is hard. Part of growing up for most of us is becoming socially conditioned. Sadly, we are taught to adhere rigidly to other people's ideas and ways of doing things. Conditioning is supposed to make life simpler, but it makes it harder because it silences our innate wisdom.

In order to come back into the flow of our life, we need to uncover our conditioned beliefs and then follow the path of *least* resistance. Reiki can help!

As we will discuss later, living in flow does not mean there is no commitment or discipline required. Of course, you need to find the time, prioritise your Reiki practice, and make your inner journey a primary focus if you want to reap the full benefits of the practice.

Take your lessons from nature. When water flows, it takes the path already formed. It doesn't try to run uphill or move mountains when a valley already exists; it finds the natural, easy path. Travelling inwards and finding your truth is much easier than you may think.

Me Before You

Coming into inner focus requires following the "me before you" dictum. Many of my students are empathic people who feel a strong desire to help others and be of service. This is a wonderful sentiment and also a double-edged sword. Empathy means having the *ability to share another person's feelings and emotions as if they were your own*.

Healthy empathy enables us to feel compassion, a form of unconditional love. You understand how other people are feeling, you can imagine walking in their shoes, and these things give you an ability to speak to them from their positions. At the same time, you also have a strong sense of self. You realize that you are not them, and you are not walking in their shoes—although you can understand other people's issues, you are not confused that you have the same ones. Their issues are not your issue, and it is not your responsibility to resolve them.

If you listen deeply to any accomplished spiritual teacher, you will discover a healthy sense of self in action. When they answer generic questions, we get universal teachings, but when they answer personal questions, we get highly individualized answers that may contradict what the teacher told another person only moments earlier.

This is not the teacher being confused. This is the teacher being highly empathic.

If you are a healer or therapist, healthy empathy means you can sit with different people all day long, show them compassion, and not be drained. Like a clear mirror, you can reflect for them what needs to be seen, and once each person has gone, you are not changed. You can see everyone's point of view, but instead of being confused or easily swayed, you are steady in your inner knowing. You have a firm understanding that your own life is yours to lead and a deep understanding that the only responsibility you have is to live your life fully. You naturally take care of yourself.

The other side of empathy is less healthy. It comes into play when a poor sense of self exists. This is like the actor who uses empathy to play a role and then forgets he is merely playing a role and continues to believe he *is* the character. We often put on roles such as *mother* or *husband*, *high-flyer* or *teacher*, and then don't take the time to remember that these are just roles—they do not define us.

As a mother, I have often fallen into this mode of seeing my parental role as all I am. I have often undermined my own desires *for the greater good of my family*. Sometimes this is totally appropriate and part of the usual compromise and balance of family life. But when self-sacrifice is chronic and one-sided, it poses a very big problem for both us and the children. We begin to walk in our children's' shoes, to live through them, and to blur the boundaries between identities. I have seen some of my friends and clients face enormous pain once the children have left home or immeasurable suffering in trying to keep the children close when they want to be free. And the children feel absolutely smothered and controlled.

Our so-called empathy can turn very needy if we're not practising setting and respecting healthy boundaries. Whether in the home or the workplace, a lack of inner steadiness projects out into the world as overprotective, meddling, controlling, and clingy. When we subjugate our own needs to those of another, it may seem empathic, but in general, it ends in a loss of our identity and a burden on others to fill that void.

By contrast, when we work on our own sense of self and remember "me before you" then we can be compassionate whilst also taking care of our own inner truth.

In unhealthy empathy, it's easy to become confused and think the unhappiness of other people affects us. As sensitive beings, we may feel their sadness, of course, but it's not OK for us to forget that they have their own expression of life, just as we have ours.

It is common to believe that for us to feel OK our loved ones need to be OK. But this expectation can become a huge burden for them. What if it was OK for them to be happy or sad, OK or not OK, doing the things you wanted them to, or not?

I know from my own experience that I feel much more heard, accepted, and loved by people who are simply there for me—in whatever state I appear—than by those who express an incessant need to fix me, heal me, and make me "better." These "fixers" make me feel there is something wrong with me for thinking or feeling as I do, and I feel a burden of responsibility to change myself in order to stop their worrying. Basically, my response is the opposite of what the fixers themselves think they are doing.

If you are a parent, you know that allowing your children to suffer or to work things out for themselves is the hardest part of parenting. I am not talking about avoidable suffering or abuse, but the day-to-day, growing-up kind of things, including trusting them to work out friendship issues, learn right from wrong, make their own mistakes, and come to their own conclusions. Granted, society doesn't support us in allowing our kids to find their own feet.

I feel the burden of this just as you do—every parenting book and research paper tells us what we should or shouldn't be doing at this or that age and describes the terrible consequences that will befall our children if we deviate. But we also must recognize that every new generation grows up in a world alien to that of the parents. Our upbringing—using our own childhoods as reference points—is not a helpful compass. Our children grow up with completely different challenges, just as we did, as compared with our parents.

What I have found to be true is that when I focus on myself and my own steadiness and happiness, my children are more likely to come to me with their issues, and I am more likely to respond to them and the needs and concerns they express from a loving and caring place. When I am busy trying to make them OK, so that I can be OK, the conversations are controlling, limiting, and usually end in arguments and even more unhappiness.

Paradoxically, the more you focus on yourself, the more you can be of service to others. The more you take care of your own burdens, the less you burden others. The more you love yourself the more others can feel your love. Helping yourself first is a critical principle of any spiritual journey.

Honestly, this is where many of us struggle for years; it is so ingrained in our beliefs and cultures that placing "me before you" is selfish and wrong. But in order to truly find out who you are, you must be willing to look and be honest, without constant self-judgment and imagining what others will think about you, or what they need from you.

The world, your loved ones, and your life desperately need you to take heart and be willing to be first.

"Me First," as Service to Others

A beautiful thing happens when you focus on yourself and the things you are passionate about—you become happy and fulfilled. You have a radiance that shines from within you and inspires others. You have much more capacity to give to others because you yourself are full of life.

It also can be motivating to dedicate your self-care to the service of others. Seen this way, your inner journey and happiness are of utmost importance to the wellbeing of the planet. It is obvious what humanity's unhappiness is doing to the planet: It is destroying it. Your commitment to your spiritual journey is in part a commitment not to add to the destruction. Shining with the light of inner truth gives others permission to do the same.

I practice self-love because then I can be in harmony, and in a state of harmony, I emit love and peace and all the things I wish for the world.

My replenishment gives me more capacity to support others. By doing Reiki, I heal myself and become more available to the people in my world. Could I help and support my loved ones if I myself were exhausted, ill, or frustrated? Could I help bring peace and happiness into the world if I myself were feeling fed up and angry? No, I couldn't.

The inner commitment to our spiritual practice is an important pact we make with ourselves to stay true to ourselves or to find ourselves again if we get lost. It is a commitment to tending to ourselves first so that what we project outwards is true service to others and not a burden—particularly behaviour that superficially looks like service, but is in fact neediness, lack of steadiness, or misplaced empathy.

As you read this book, you will see that, ultimately, everything is connected. Deciding to use Reiki primarily as a spiritual practice is such an important decision to make. If you do, you will be adding a level of sacred intention that you may have felt was missing before. With this decision, you will be agreeing that following your own inner path is more important than following what everyone else wants you to do. You will be agreeing that living your own life and finding your flow is more important than keeping other people happy or making them comfortable.

The great thing about this is that by following your own path, you give others permission to do the same—and this makes a difference. If one person gives permission to a hundred others, those hundred may then shine permission to another 10,000, and so on. It wouldn't take many people following their truth to affect the entire planetary population positively. Stepping into Reiki as a spiritual path is truly your contribution not only to Reiki but to raising the consciousness of everyone on this planet.

I look at it as simple arithmetic. My Reiki practice adds to your Reiki practice.

PART II
The Reiki Spiritual Path

I started teaching Reiki in 1995 at the young age of twenty-eight. I was working in advertising and the most spiritual thing going on in my life at the time was "girls' night" —a lot of spirits were consumed! I practised and taught Reiki from the extreme relative viewpoint—Reiki and I were totally different entities. My classes were full of people like me, not surprisingly—people looking for a quick fix, a "bliss out," people looking for a way to "fuel up" and get on with life.

Ten years went by and I noticed the students I attracted changing over time. These students came in wanting more, they wanted to help themselves to heal. They were not looking for a quick fix but a long-term solution. Another ten years of watching students heal and grow and I noticed an entirely different student appearing: the spiritual seeker. Along the way I noticed a very close correlation between my own spiritual development and the students appearing before me. They say "When the student is ready, the teacher appears" and in my experience it is equally true "When the teacher is ready, the student appears"!

The following stages I outline as the Reiki spiritual path is more accurately *my* spiritual path and the path of many of my students. Over the years, I have been blessed with the most fantastic Reiki community, many of my students become my lifelong friends and Reiki master peers, so I have had the privilege of watching them on their spiritual journeys too. The stages unfold with uncanny similarities, so much so that I often tell new Reiki students that this will happen, then this, then this—in this order—and they report back that indeed it did. When we gather for our annual Reiki teacher conference you can almost plot a graph along the spiritual path outlined here with each teacher based on no more than the years they have been teaching, and how prolifically. In other words, there is a strong correlation between how experienced a person is with their Reiki tools, and their spiritual growth.

Of course, this is not a hard and fast rule. Not all experienced Reiki teachers see Reiki as a spiritual path. But if they do, the correlation is striking in its general trajectory.

I hope this observation gives you confidence that this path is well-trodden and certainly effective. The more you use the tools, the further along you will travel, assuming you are deliberately using Reiki as a spiritual path.

Here in Part II, let us turn our attention to the four stages of this path.

> **Stage 1.** Turning our attention inwards and becoming sensitive to our inner truth
> **Stage 2.** Deconditioning the mind and uncovering the layers of confusion
> **Stage 3.** Minding the gap between our thoughts and seeing our true nature
> **Stage 4.** Living life purposefully and without conditions

It's important to realize that as you master the first stage of awareness, you don't forgo it when you move on! You incorporate the stages as you master them so that all four become one whole. Each stage of the path is a foundation that is essential for the next, and that foundation is essential for the next, and so on. Spiritual development is like building a pyramid, the base must be broad and wide. You cannot take away the foundation and expect subsequent stages to remain stable. Eventually, the essences of the four stages begin to balance and merge.

At the first two stages of the spiritual path, it is easy to stop. A certain relief comes when you begin to dismantle your mental and emotional conditioning. You become much happier in your body, you feel more self-love, and you are more aligned with the flow of your life. But you still see yourself as a separate entity and Reiki as something outside you.

Not only is it easy to halt your progress here, I would say that most Reiki students stop here. They use Reiki for relief from their suffering, but don't realise the truth of what they have. Reiki can be like a comforting blanket to wrap around yourself when you feel weary, distressed, ill, or depressed, as it lifts you out of that feeling and into more pleasant ones. But like any symptom, you will fall back into distress until you arrive at stage three. Until you can perceive the absolute truth that you are, in fact, Reiki, you will never have lasting peace or freedom.

Seeing your true nature, that you are the awareness and not your thoughts is a paradigm shift. It comes as a huge relief and can be another point where people stop. The enormous freedom of being disconnected from your burdensome and tyrannical beliefs can be more than enough for many people, and yet living your life in the gaps is still not completion. It just means you have swung from one end of the pendulum to the other side.

So, keep going. Don't stop. At the final stage you can see the whole picture, you are your thoughts, you are the gaps, and you are the life force itself expressing as your purpose. All parts of you are welcome and perfectly complete.

At the last stage, you realise that there is never any stopping, there is resting for sure, there is no more struggle and there is enthusiasm and creative joyfulness. But the deepening continues, into infinity. Life is evolving to know itself, and there is no full stop to that.

The next five chapters explore the progression of development you can anticipate experiencing, and you will recognise many parts of this journey, as you are already on it. The call of this book is to keep going, do not stop, enlighten yourself to yourself, and find your freedom.

6. Turning Attention Inwards

> *Without courage, we cannot practice any other virtue with consistency. We can't be kind, true, merciful, generous, or honest.*
>
> —Maya Angelou

The spiritual journey is, in many ways, a hero's journey. It requires immense courage to face inwards when the rest of the world faces out. By taking this path, you will go against the grain of society, against what most people deem appropriate. Frankly, you probably will piss people off.

Following your own life path is a singular journey, it is for the solo traveller. You have ditched the safe package tour in favour of freedom, with all the trials and rewards that this kind of travelling entails. You have to figure out and manage the foreign terrain, and you also get to experience a richer and more self-directed journey.

Although you may feel estranged from other people by going solo, a major benefit of the journey is that you no longer need to feel estranged from yourself.

Many of us feel disempowered in our lives until we enter a spiritual path because we have been coerced and brainwashed since childhood to "do the right thing," and then we bully ourselves to continue adhering to beliefs and structures that do not serve our personal truth. We have never questioned what is true for us until now. And it's an empowering question.

To truly step into our own power we need to be committed to our inner world and this takes place over stages. First we need to move our attention from the outside world of things and how we relate to them. Next, become alert to what is coming up mentally, emotionally, and physically inside our body.

Going inwards instead of projecting our attention outwards is not what we are taught to do in the western world. We are taught that the pursuit of happiness (note the word *pursuit*) entails finding the perfect partner/job/environment/friends. We are taught that success is measured in money or fame. It's habitual to keep striving for and pursuing results externally in order to quiet the internal dissatisfaction. We are so conditioned that we naturally blame everything that we perceive is wrong with us and our lives in the outside world. When we look around, adhering to this strategy of external pursuit of happiness is what everyone else seems to agree we need to do.

Stepping into our own power generally requires us to leave the well-trodden "how we should all live life" path and strike out on our own "how I want to live my life" path. It means getting off the tour bus. The rest of the world may be on the exhausting sixteen-countries-in-thirty-days tour herding around for Instagramable shots, but that doesn't mean it's what you want to do.

When we leave the tour, we essentially strike out on our own adventure into the great unknown. This sets us up for resistance from those around us, which may sound a lot like our own self-doubts. Our choices may now set us apart from what most of our family and friends think of as normal or correct. In the beginning, it's a tough endeavour to be different. It's really no wonder only a handful of us heed the inner calling! But it's worth it.

Once you begin to journey, you will meet many other solo travellers and many communities who help empower and encourage you. Solo travellers love to meet others and they honour and appreciate your own journey far more genuinely than the tour bus pack. Finding a community that supports and understands your own journey can be incredibly helpful and so much exists now both online and through events and meetings.

I recently did some solo travelling around Europe as a little adventure. I had a general itinerary planned out. I saw all the major sights (and took all the Instagram photos!), but I also had days where I would just go walking. Without fail, the walking days were highlights on my trip. One day I discovered a beautiful house museum, another day a fabulous church, and I had the most enriching, almost mystical experiences on the days I simply allowed to unfold by themselves. It was so magical, and I would have never seen or experienced any of it on a tour bus.

When you go solo travelling, everything is more up close and personal. You need to be more alert and aware because no one else is organising you or telling you where to go. You make your own choices, and you have the freedom to just get up and go wherever life takes you.

The Answers Are Within Us

The Reiki spiritual path is the journey to self-discovery: *Who am I?* This cannot be explored in the outward pursuit of happiness. The first step of this inward journey is to explore the correct environment: our body. Let's use an analogy to explore this concept.

Imagine going to a doctor because you have a fever and he gives you a thermometer to go check the temperature of your house. This is what we are doing with our happiness, time and time again: We feel unhappy and check the world outside for the cause without ever exploring our inner world. Checking our relationships, our career, our home, our bank account is as insane as checking the temperature of our house and treating that instead of the fever in our body.

You need to look at the fever first and assess: What is the true cause of this? Maybe it is the temperature of your house, maybe it is a pathogen in your body, or maybe it is alerting you to a deeper issue. Perhaps it's time to take off your thermal underwear.

The spiritual journey is looking inwards, asking questions, finding the answer out for yourself, and this requires a deep sensitivity to the body. The body never lies, and when it is trying to tell you something, it will tense up, create pain or illness, or give you sleepless nights and unexplainable symptoms. Probably the reason you began your Reiki journey was that your body was out of balance in some way physically, emotionally, or mentally. The body called you to Reiki and it is the key to building trust in your inner wisdom at stage one of your spiritual development.

To *heal* is to "make whole." Even with the smallest amount of reflection, it should be clear that healing must be an inside job. Although we have been brainwashed to believe that everyone else knows better, it's simply not possible when it comes to our reality. How can someone else know more about you than you do?

Building trust in yourself means taking healing into your own hands. And that makes it a huge responsibility—because it means you don't just go running to someone else when things get difficult but sit with whatever is coming up and investigate it yourself. If you decide to go to someone else for a second opinion, you don't abdicate your responsibility for your wellbeing by assuming whatever the other person says to you is true. Keep your common sense, keep your autonomy, and connect to your own inner truth. Life is an inside job, and no one can ever know you better than you know yourself. It is not possible, not ever.

If we continue with the fever analogy, perhaps it is the first time you have ever had a fever, so it may be appropriate to get a second opinion. You go to the doctor and he tells you to adjust the temperature of the house. You may wonder about the efficacy of this advice, but he's the expert, so you do as he says. You adjust the temperature of the house, and then notice the fever remains. Perhaps the doctor insists you need to keep adjusting the house temperature until you find the proper heat for your body. As you adjust and adjust and notice no change to your fever, you may also notice an arising of the question in your mind: *What else might it be?*

You could go in different directions with this question, you could continue to ask more and more experts and collect more and more opinions, or you could begin your own inward exploration—and ask the fever itself.

This inwards and outwards search for answers is very commonplace in the beginning. Every time you hit a new issue you may be tempted to go to an expert. But over time (if you direct your attention inwards), you will go directly to the issue with more and more confidence. You will be able to ask the fever directly, and you will be able to hear its answer.

In the beginning, depending on how deeply disempowered you have been until now, asking the right question and hearing the inner answers can be difficult. The amount of junk filling our heads is shocking. How to discern the junk from the truth? If you have spent decades asking others and following their answers, this first step on the path can be extremely confusing.

Fortunately, that is where Reiki self-treatment comes in. It is your gateway to greater discernment and inner connection with your truth—which are both necessary if your intent is to follow your own path and live in flow with life force.

Why Is Self-Treatment So Important?

Self-treatment is the key to self-empowerment—it's really one and the same thing.

As we open to the flow of Reiki, we allow balancing to happen. Reiki helps us feel better, more balanced, and calmer and we do it ourselves, not with the help of experts. When we first begin our Reiki journey, this is groundbreaking. We can help ourselves! We have the capacity to rejuvenate, to balance, to settle ourselves! This discovery is the first important step to self-empowerment. It is so compelling that we start looking inwards instead of outwards for answers. Maybe we have the answers within ourselves? Maybe we really do know what is best for us, and we have the power to give it to ourselves. Maybe instead of asking everyone else I should ask myself?

The first important reason for self-treatment is to develop trust that we can heal ourselves.

The self-treatment is also an invitation to be with yourself—and listen. It is a meditation and a conscious shift of attention from the busyness of doing and achieving things to the quiet reflection of what we are experiencing in our own body. Self-treatment is the reminder that the answer to *who am I?* is not outside in the world of things, but inside our body.

The second important reason for self-treatment is to practice directing our attention inwards.

As we practise, we become aware of an underlying peaceful presence that exists within us. The more we connect with this presence the more we become aware that it is always there, even when we feel upset or anxious. It may take us a while to feel its consistency, and it may be much easier to feel it when we are doing our self-treatments then when we are busy in our life. But self-treatments build not only our awareness of this presence, but also a stronger connection with it over time.

The third important reason for self-treatment is to connect with our true nature.

You may already have a self-treatment regime that has served you for years, so as you read on also be looking at how to deepen your experience. Perhaps you are already very committed to a daily practice, but what are you doing with this time? Are you daydreaming in your head or are you directing your attention inwards into your body? As you experiment and explore and become more aware of what is happening in your body, you will notice that what you are thinking affects the body. I notice that when I am busy in my head telling myself a story about this person or that incident, my body actually tenses up. If I am sitting and doing my Reiki, I notice my shoulders start to tighten upwards, my neck protrudes forwards as if my head is trying to "get ahead" of my body, and this produces pain and poor posture.

Years of chiropractic therapy have taught me how to maintain good posture: My neck should be coming straight up, out of my shoulders (not craning forward), my shoulders should be relaxed, and my shoulder blades tucked in a downwards direction with my sternum slightly raised, not collapsed into my chest. I know this is the best way to relieve my shoulder tension and neck pain, yet I can only remember to maintain this, and the resultant relief of pain and tension good posture provides, when I am not babbling away some nonsense to myself in my head.

When you begin to observe this kind of mind/body interaction it becomes very helpful for your spiritual growth, because ultimately, we want to spend less and less time in our narrative, and more and more time in our bodies. Lifeforce and your connection with it is through your body, not through your thoughts.

Commitment to Our Inner World

Commitment to doing regular Reiki self-treatments comes in two forms: commitment to spending an hour or so on your inner practice, and commitment to focused observation of the thoughts and feelings that come up during that hour.

Finding the Time to Practise

It tends to take about twenty minutes of Reiki practice for the mind to quiet down, which it does all by itself—but you must be willing to go through the process of getting this far! Quick five- to ten-minute Reiki treatments are not going to give you this effect. This is why your commitment is key.

You need to know: Are you looking for inner peace or a magic pill? Are you looking for your inner truth, wisdom, and connection with life or temporary comfort? These are important questions to ask yourself, as a regular and lengthy self-treatment is what is required to gain the benefits of Reiki practise. An hour a day in deep reflection and inner communion will change your life.

When the mind is quiet and not running an extravagant movie in our heads, the most extraordinary wisdom and inner connection arise—but you will never see this until you allow the mind to shut up! When I first embarked on Reiki self-treatments, my mind was a chaotic, frustrating mess. But miraculously, each time I did a one-hour treatment I would notice a quieting after about twenty minutes. Not a complete silence, but a quieting. The thoughts that flowed in and out of my mind appeared less contracted, less important. I was able to loosen my attachment to believing them and create space around them. Relaxing the consistent contraction and just feel peaceful.

You will have had this same feeling—a deep sense of peace. It is in this peace that your autonomy lives. This peace is your true nature.

If every day, day by day, you go into a space of quiet, a space of peace, it becomes more extended. You begin to loosen in all aspects of your life, to relax more and more, and to stop seeing your mind as all there is of you. You expand into the great vast spaciousness that is the real you. You begin to see your life in a totally new and freer way. All this from a simple hour-a-day routine!

Getting started with the time commitment is the tough part. My students often tell me they don't have time to carve out the one hour necessary. It's a priority issue for them at this stage of spiritual development; their *doing* is still more important to them than their *being*. But their priority shifts if they persist in showing up for the regular self-treatment.

Once we've achieved enough things, tried and failed to change enough things, and tried and failed to control enough circumstances in our life, we start to realize that the *doing* is never enough, we are never fulfilled, and we are constantly chasing the next doing. Once we see we're on a never-ending and exhausting hamster wheel, we can get off.

Finding the New Direction

The critical shift that occurs at this stage is from an external focus to internal focus. You must make this shift in order to willingly carve out the time needed to explore your inner experience. Both the time and the direction are important, and it doesn't matter which you find first. I often joke that I was "blessed with insomnia," as this meant finding an hour every night was easy for me. I would go to bed and lie in bed for hours anyway, so why not play some soothing music and do my Reiki practice?

What I noticed very quickly was how powerful this regular self-treatment was to my wellbeing, fixing my insomnia in a matter of weeks. My own commitment came via circumstance and, lucky for me, once insomnia eased, I already knew what I had in my hands and I was not going to stop for any reason!

My commitment to looking inwards for answers took much longer to come about. For years I was doing my self-treatment exclusively because of the physical and mental relief it brought me. Reiki self-treatment helped me sleep. It helped my immune system. It relieved my stress. My practice had no intent to self-discover; it was more for escape—from my stress, the world, my worries. I was blanketing myself in Reiki for the relief; I wasn't actively looking inwards or seeing what was going on—or asking anything of my practice. When peace and harmony came to me, I didn't investigate them, see where they were coming from, wonder if they were self-generated. I simply assumed that Reiki was "doing it" for me. This one big myth, if you bust any of them, is the important one.

Most people begin their self-treatment with this myth: *Reiki is doing it for me.* With this belief in mind, we permit ourselves to zone out when we do our self-treatment. We are not mindful, and we do not treat it as a meditation practice. People think they are practising Reiki, yet they are not utilizing the power of it to nearly its full potential.

We do the same with meditation and yoga, we have dumbed down all these sacred and powerful practices to make our lives more comfortable, but this just puts a Band-Aid over the dissatisfaction. It never brings real freedom.

When you realize that *where* you place your attention is the key to your freedom, you begin to spend more and more time taking care of that. Then finding time for self-treatment becomes easy, it's just an essential part of coming into inner ease and peace with yourself—and the more you do it, the more you value it.

With Reiki as your spiritual path, self-treatment becomes your meditation. If you already do meditation, you can bring all your techniques into your Reiki practice and blend them whichever way suits you. The beauty of Reiki is its lack of rigid form. Design your own practice so that it works for you. All that is needed is a commitment to look.

And although finding the time is a key component to your commitment, there is a bigger component, which is *how* you are spending that time. Anyone who spends the time on self-treatment will get benefits, but the full potential of what is available will only emerge if you spend your time *mindfully*.

Be Alert to the Process

When you don't take the time to understand the body and its sensations, and how your thoughts control you, you will never be free. The body can be tense and upset, while you are in your mind telling yourself everything is fine. We do this all the time: We negate what our bodies tell us. We ignore the signals, and then we wonder why we are not happy or comfortable in our own skins.

But if you can't reside in your own body and understand yourself fully, how can you be comfortable? Something will always sneak up when you feel vulnerable and knock you off your feet.

Being fully and firmly grounded in your body is the only way to be free. You cannot escape through the crown chakra. You cannot distract yourself into bliss. You can try, but it won't last. Your only route to freedom is via the body. And ironically, once you make friends with it, it is your greatest ally and never lies to you. You can trust your body implicitly.

When you are doing your self-treatment, be in your body. What pain or tension resides in the body? How does your body feel? How does the Reiki feel in your hands and in your body? Get really present with yourself—not in your head, daydreaming, but in the body—with your breath, your sensations, and your thoughts as they arise. Not running away with them and then forgetting what you are doing.

During a typical self-treatment, you will go through various stages of deepening. Do your best to become familiar with them. At what point do you zone out and forget what you are doing? At what point does your mind take over and daydream? Do you even catch yourself? For most of us, being present and aware is impossible to do consistently for a long period of time. In the beginning, we may only stay present for thirty seconds before our minds take us on a merry-go-round of thinking. But if we stay mindful and gently bring ourselves back to the hands, to the bodily sensations, then over time we get better and better, quieter and quieter.

During the process of any self-treatment, we go through many layers. It's common to spend the first ten to twenty minutes with our busy minds. If we persevere through this stage, we get to a quieter place—this is where many of us fall asleep, zone out, or start daydreaming.

See if you can shift your direction once you arrive in the quiet space. Make observations. Inquire. Under all the thoughts, what exists? You will likely notice a sense of wellbeing, peace, awareness. Focus your attention on this spaciousness, and simply rest. When you bring your attention to this space and deliberately rest in it—not in your busy mind—you will see your true nature. This awareness (this "me-ness") is all you need to see. It is always with you.

The most common feeling you will get when you do your Reiki practice is deep inner peace, but have you ever explored the peace itself? Apart from the relief of feeling peaceful, or the gratitude you have for it, have you ever taken time to look at it? Or asked: From where does it arise? Whose peace is it? Does it come and go or is it always present? When you are alert to the process and see the process itself as an exploration, an entirely new dimension opens.

What happens when you experience discomfort or resistance? Maybe memories of old trauma, boredom or irritation. Maybe uncomfortable or intense body sensations. If we see Reiki as a relief from these uncomfortable feelings, then we will stop, get up, and do something else. If we see these experiences as something to observe, to get acquainted with, we will persist and see what is under them. Remembering that you cannot find lasting freedom until you are willing to travel through all your conditioned layers should help you to remain steady and keep going.

Getting Comfortable with Uncomfortable Feelings

Although we are lucky that Reiki treatments usually feel very loving and supportive, we get down into the murkier depths of our inner lives sooner or later. If you run from the first sign of discomfort when this happens for you, it is a chance to simply stop and reflect on why you are doing that. What are your beliefs around life, experiences, and spiritual growth in general? Are you expecting your spiritual progress to be measured only in good feelings?

If you reflect on your biggest learning moments, they are usually quite painful or challenging. Naturally, when you deepen with Reiki, there are going to be moments when things feel very uncomfortable. You may detox, or release, extremely uncomfortable emotions or memories. You may come face to face with darker parts of yourself that you really don't want to see. But remember, we benefit when we are willing to sit with anything that comes up, good or bad, and simply observe or meet it with compassion. Then the blockage can release, or the imbalance has a chance to balance itself.

If we keep resisting and running from our thoughts and feelings, all that happens is that we continue to hold them tightly in our system, and this eventually leads to illness or pain, and mental/emotional stress or anxiety. Getting comfortable in our bodies requires us to be willing to accept all parts of our experience, including trauma and rage.

Most of us hold considerable unresolved trauma from our early lives in our systems, even if we have had relatively peaceful or happy childhoods. Growing up is simply a traumatic experience! We are vulnerable and easily thrown off course because we are easily affected by strong emotions that come from others.

When an uncomfortable emotion, childhood memory, or constricted belief system comes to light, the key to healing is just to accept it as it comes: *Ah, look! There is a memory of how hurt I was as a child when my mother said this or that to me, Oh, I remember my fear when this or that happened to me.* In doing so, we can "re-member" (reintegrate) ourselves as we recall the experience, harmonise with it, and give it a place in our energy system.

Shoving an uncomfortable feeling into the basement or banishing it to the back of our mind does not restore our harmony—rather, like a bee in an enclosed space, it gets loud and angry. Neither should we try to release it by force, getting rid of it just so that it no longer bothers us. Acceptance and compassion are what is needed from us, not fear and resistance. Open to it all. It is all you after all.

What I have also found is that what we sometimes think of as a release is still only resistance disguised as a releasing technique! Often when I am faced with a particularly painful memory or emotion, I jump straight to my preferred releasing technique—whether it's breathing, yoga, reciting a mantra, or distilling my favourite aromatherapy oils—rather than go through the first step of acknowledging and accepting the memory or emotion.

This is the blessing of the self-treatment protocol—you are stuck with it! If you commit to the hour and don't get up or stop every time you feel uncomfortable, what you will notice is that if something uncomfortable comes up and you stay with it, it passes.

Maybe you need to cry or shake as it passes. Maybe you need to scream into the pillow. Whatever happens—it always passes. This is a very powerful realization to have. Once you fully realize this, uncomfortable feelings, in general, loosen their hold on you, as you can be with them without pushing them away, knowing they will pass in their own time.

Accept, Accept, Accept

Often people confuse acceptance with agreement. But acceptance is not agreement—it does not mean you have to agree that when your father hurt you it was OK, or when you got abandoned it was deserved. It is not about agreeing that anything is OK. It's about simply accepting that it happened, and it hurt, and you didn't enjoy it. Getting clear on the difference between acceptance and agreement is an important lesson at this stage.

Another confusion that often occurs is the idea that we must "fix it." Well, maybe, if your father is still hurting you, then it's time to say no. But if it is a thing from the past, how are you going to fix it? There is nothing to fix here and now. Only an opportunity for acknowledgement: *Yes, this happened to me, it hurt, and now I can see the hurt more clearly and bring it fully into my awareness.*

Recently, I have been working on clearing some very deeply buried emotional trauma. I have become so good at meditating, yoga, and self-Reiki that the only hint that there was even trauma in the body was, of course, the body. I was experiencing a very tight jaw and a low-grade tension running throughout my body. It had been like this for years, and as I have a very tall and slim frame, I've come to accept that my physiology just doesn't hold itself well together. But there were other things—outbursts of anger, sudden feelings of intense sadness, bouts of insomnia. I had good reasons to justify all these symptoms (including planetary alignments and Mercury retrogrades!), and it was only when I was talking to a very alert therapist that she pointed out what I was saying and what she was feeling from me seemed out of sync.

And she was totally right. When I stopped midsentence to become quiet and alert to what my body was feeling, I noticed intense emotional tightness in my chest. In fact, I had almost been holding my breath as I chattered on about this and that. Honestly, it was shocking to me that, after all my inner work, I was still side-stepping painful experiences and deep trauma. Because I am skilful, my inner work had given me even more techniques to hide behind!

Alertness is not only valuable during Reiki self-treatment, but also in general. When you are talking and interacting with others, be vigilant to the inner expressions of your body. Notice when it gets upset and tight, when you stop breathing, or the breathing pattern changes. See if you can drop into the body more and feel what it is trying to bring up to the light.

In my case, it took months for the very deep suppression of the buried memories to begin to release, and for the longest time, I felt myself circling the pain, peeking inside and then swiftly disengaging back into my head with my stories, my explanations, and my excuses. It's amazing the defence mechanisms we have in place—and probably for a good reason. There is always a benefit to the way we protect ourselves from trauma or distress. Denial helps us cope when there are no other options. It helps us deal with stressful life situations until a calmer or more appropriate time presents itself.

The key to healing is staying alert for the timing when the body feels safe enough to begin to show you its deeper distress. It takes an enormous amount of courage and trust in both yourself and your body to go deep into pain.

In my case, I had to come into a very intimate space with the pain, and also to contend with my unwillingness to stay in it too long. Being alert is not judging how alert you are or how fast you are able to move into awareness. Alertness is simply alertness: *I am feeling pain. I am moving away from pain.* These extremes and anything between them are perfect and fine.

Nothing to Fix or Change

What I found during this self-exploration was that there is a very subtle balance between accepting and fixing. This trauma was not new to me. In fact, I had circled around healing it many times before, crying and releasing many times before. So, what was different this time? What I noticed was a non-judgmental quality in myself when I was present to it that was altogether softer and more observant. If I am brutally honest with myself, the previous attempts at releasing had been exactly that: attempts to release. I had been trying to get rid of the uncomfortable feelings and memories instead of accepting them.

This is a critical point of distinction that you must play with experientially to see for yourself. As with all concepts pointed at in this book, you must experience and know it for yourself, in your own body, for it to be helpful. For release to happen, for real, you need paradoxically to go into the experience without any agenda to get rid of it. I know you may have heard this comment before, but do not use the familiarity to dismiss it. Hearing it said (or reading it in a book) and experiencing it is very different.

Why? Among other things, the experience enlightens you about the reason why all the other attempts you made didn't work. When we have an agenda, no matter how hidden and unconscious, the agenda itself is what stops the release. The agenda itself is the resistance to acknowledging and accepting the trauma, and so it gets driven further underground.

On the surface, you may feel like you have released. I certainly fooled myself for many years. But the body keeps hold of it, and you know this because the body doesn't feel at ease, there is no lasting peace.

Being alert is being curious with everything that you discover internally and doing it with compassion—you are not using what you see to beat yourself up, as this would be just more madness. You are looking with gentle clarity, not from your head but from your body—and your senses. What is happening in your hands during a self-treatment? What are your bodily sensations? How is your breath? Every time you notice your critical thoughts or ruminations, gently bring yourself back to your body and its sensations. Your mind really has nothing productive to offer you at this point in the journey—and only your body needs attention.

When you notice unpleasant thoughts, feelings, or emotions arising during your Reiki self-treatment, remember there is nothing to fix. Hold the unpleasantness. Try to bring the emotions closer, not further away, and then simply acknowledge what you already know. There will be no surprises—you are already aware of your sadness, your grief, your anger. The stories are already rattling around your head and body. These thoughts and feelings are no strangers to you, although the intensity may be, the depth of feeling may be—after all you've been running or pushing or resisting them for years.

Instead, stop. Be alert, compassionate, open, and courageous. You will surprise yourself. I promise.

You may come into a stage of either boredom or avoidance—this can come in the form of falling asleep or becoming increasingly bored and irritated with lying still. This is progress! Boredom is the doorway to insight. When I notice I am bored or becoming irritated with wasting my time doing Reiki, I become even more alert and curious. I ask: *What is this I am hitting up against? What is it I am trying to hide away from? What is behind the boredom? What lurks so unconsciously that I must fall asleep to avoid it?* You may continue like this for days, or even weeks, but with persistence and commitment it will eventually dissolve under your insistent, yet gentle curiosity.

What arises from behind the boredom will always surprise you.

Sincerity and Ego

Sincerity is the willingness to be honest. When we notice the body is tense or uneasy, are we willing to ask why? Do we try to find an explanation? Do we jump to blame someone/something for our tension? Do we try out different techniques to get rid of it? Are we willing to feel bad as well as good? Are we willing to consider that we may be in denial about something painful?

Sincerity is in expressing the courage to look within—and this includes the good, the bad, and the ugly. Are you willing to take a clear look at yourself and how you cause your own suffering? Are you willing to admit to your bad deeds and unkind words? Are you willing to acknowledge your misery or discomfort? Unless you can acknowledge all your actions and all your feelings as part of your life experience you cannot feel whole, avoiding or denying the bad or ugly parts of yourself means their energy cannot integrate and they will be forever rattling around your energy system as resistance and blame.

The flip side of sincerity is judgement. Judgement is deciding whether you think something is correct or not, it puts your ego into a superior position of "knowing better" than whatever is being judged. It may be another person, it may be a situation, more commonly it is yourself. When you notice judgement creeping into your thoughts *(You should have done this or that, they shouldn't have done this or that)*, it tends to be a gift. It is a useful red flag. When we project it outwards it is the egos way of deflecting behaviour, we ourselves are engaged in. We feel uncomfortable with this behaviour and so we "get rid of it" by projecting our feelings outwards by finding someone else to judge, someone who does the same things we do, but "does it worse" than us. This is a very subtle form of denial that can easily go unnoticed.

Often when I am sitting and doing my Reiki self-treatments my mind will wander off, and I will find myself thinking about certain people; and then, without consciously meaning to, I find myself judging certain behaviours or things they have said. When I am mindful, I am grateful to catch these incidences of judgement. They hold immense wisdom because the thing I am judging the other person for is usually the very thing I am trying to escape noticing in myself.

When people hear this, they will often react with, "No, that's not me! I judge murderers as bad people, but I have never murdered anyone!" Have you ever murdered anything? An ant? A mosquito? An idea? As I said, we look for people to judge who are much more extreme, this is part of the smokescreen of the ego. If you judge murderers as evil and wrong, I guarantee you there is a part of you that judges your own murdering ways. When you can forgive yourself for all the murder you have committed in your life, you will notice you have much more compassion for those who murder on a larger scale.

And please don't take this the wrong way, I am not condoning murder! There is the ethical right and wrong judgement that helps guide our outlook on life, and there is the "all riled up and ranting and raving" judgment. It is the latter I am referring too, the kind that grips your mind and creates cyclical and exhausting thoughts and stories in your head.

All judgment of this type is self-judgment. When we project it outwards, the gift is that it is easier to spot. When we are gossiping and complaining about someone else, it is easier to see the exact quality or action we find so abhorrent. Take this irritation and annoyance you feel and make it your meditation. If you think someone is horrible for lying to you, take time to reflect on all the times in your life when you yourself have lied. When you think about these occasions, does it bring you guilt and shame? Then forgive yourself, see that you are no better or no worse than the person you judge.

We are all human. When we practice this depth of sincerity and honesty with ourselves, it is super important to do so with compassion. We can be our own worst critics, and sincerity cannot exist where there is judgment. Why would you be honest if you knew you would berate yourself for the effort?

Are you willing to see how you are always doing your best? Given the number of old beliefs and rigid patterns we all hold in our systems, and that the source of many of these patterns is our parents, our culture, our society, it's amazing we are not totally paralyzed! Could we use sincerity to stay steady and to keep deepening, to keep courageously growing, and to love ourselves?

Being Willing to See Where You Are

When I was eighteen, I went to my first self-empowerment workshop and learnt to catch a ball. It seems such a silly thing, but it's often the small things that have a massive impact. All my life up until then I had held the belief *I can't catch*, and my life experience had proved it. I was always picked last for ball sports and I fumbled and dropped anything anyone tried to throw to me. I was terrified of getting involved in ball sports for fear of being humiliated.

At this self-empowerment workshop, I was told not to focus on catching the ball, but to tell the instructor which way the rings on the ball were moving—clockwise or anticlockwise. As I was intently watching the ball, I caught it with ease. I realized at that moment that for years I had instinctively squeezed my eyes shut every time something was thrown to me; I hadn't wanted to see it. This revelation shocked me into a deep and ongoing search for the truth. For eighteen years, I had believed with every fibre of my body that I couldn't catch, and in thirty seconds, this illusion had been shattered.

What else did I believe that wasn't true?

Many decades later, I am still uncovering entrenched beliefs that are not true, and with the deepening of my self-understanding, there is also growing compassion for the misunderstanding that lies in all of us. So many wounds and traumas, so much unnecessary suffering. Sometimes the hardest part at the beginning stage of the spiritual path is simply seeing the victim in you.

Beware of Skipping Stages of Spiritual Development

Often when we come to Reiki, it is to get rid of discomfort, not to embrace it! It's easy to try and skip this stage of accepting and acknowledging all parts of us and move right past into the manifesting stage—sending Reiki to this and that to try and shift the discomfort as quickly as possible. But if we bypass this step in the inner work, we only push rejected experiences and feelings deeper into our systems, where they will need to be tended to later.

Maybe that is well and good. There is a timing to all of it. But maybe you can rest on the step you're on, be more patient and thorough, and really spend awhile feeling into the aspect of you that is victimized, wounded, and grieving. Just accepting that part of you is a victim, and feeling victimized, can be a huge step in integration and healing. Approaching that part of you gently and with compassion is a critical step in this process. If you have been a healer, a Reiki teacher, or a therapist for many years, this can be extremely difficult to admit, I know it was for me. But there is no release without authentic acceptance. This level of acceptance happens intimately, deep in the body. This wounded part of you exists, and it is yearning for the light of day, to be heard, to be seen, and to be acknowledged. Do your best to embrace and nurture it.

My first wake-up experience, when I caught the ball with such ease because I had my eyes open and I was curious if it was spinning clockwise or anticlockwise, has been my spiritual metaphor. When am I squeezing my eyes tightly closed? Can I be open and curious instead? And note that when I first caught that ball, there was no self-talk. I was simply looking to see if the ball was turning clockwise or anticlockwise. I wasn't berating myself. I wasn't telling myself I couldn't do it. I wasn't fearful that a room full of people were going to laugh at my fumbling. This was exactly why I caught the ball. I wasn't listening to the debilitating self-talk. The focus was on the question, *Clockwise or anticlockwise?*

Since that day, I have always been able to catch—not in an effortless way that I see many people do it, but in a focused, look-at-the-ball-intently kind of way. I don't expect it to be easy or effortless. I know I need focus, and I need to be alert. It's practical and obvious, and there is no room for overthinking or negative self-talk. When I am open and keep it simple, I catch the ball. And when I have my eyes closed or I'm busy wondering why I can't catch better or if I'll ever be able to catch better in future, and in my head thinking about why others can catch better than me, I drop it.

In the same way, when emotions, beliefs, feelings, tensions appear during my self-practice (or anytime during the day for that matter), I ask simple questions: *What is this emotion? Where is it in my body? Can I embrace it, and rest in it awhile? Can I welcome this emotion, belief, feeling, tension, and let it out into the light of day?*

Sometimes I notice I am immediately skipping this stage and moving on to the fixing part. And that's fine too. Obviously, I'm not ready to look at whatever it is right now. Even the fact I know I am skipping and deflecting needs to be OK.

In self-enquiry, if you can embrace the attitude that there is nothing wrong and nothing to fix, it's just you, being honest with yourself. When you are sincerely interested in seeing the truth, magical things happen. Open to the possibility that all you need is right here, right now. Your next steps will arise out of your innate wisdom. Your journey will be miraculously supported.

This stage is infinite. Every day, our practice reconnects us with our inner wisdom. Our minds may find it boring or unproductive, our egos may rail against the hour spent lying down doing nothing, but in time, you will see the benefits that you derive from this commitment to yourself. You will gently open to the truth of these stages, and into an entirely different paradigm.

7. Deconditioning the Mind

Your unhappiness ultimately arises not from the circumstances of your life but from the conditioning of your mind.
—Eckhart Tolle

As we use Reiki self-treatments to travel deeper into our inner life, uncovering unhelpful belief structures, trauma, or old pain, we can use the power of intention to bring clarity and release. The self-treatment allows cultivation of mindfulness, we observe what is happening in the body, what emotions and tensions live within. And as we observe, we become aware of the underlying beliefs driving the emotions or the tension. This is where our Reiki symbols become a wonderful aid.

Sending Reiki to specific issues as they arise, or to emotional/mental blocks, allows us to laser-beam our intention resulting in a quicker and more harmonious outcome. If we imagine our inner truth as a shining lightbulb, our "big bright light," and our conditioned Google algorithms as all the dusty layers covering it, our primary job is to clean off the layers. The self-treatments help to direct our attention inwards and as we practice staying alert and getting in touch with our body, we begin to see the dust layers. Sending Reiki to these layers has the effect of cleaning them up more quickly because we are harnessing the morphic fields of the symbols.

In this chapter, my aim is to inspire ideas. Experiment with sending Reiki to layers as they come up, but also use your intention to shine the lightbulb more brightly too. We can use Reiki to not only clean up the mind's conditioning, but also to connect us more consciously with our true nature. Personally, I would greatly encourage any Reiki Level 1 student to carry on to Level 2 as a bare minimum course of study, simply for this personal growth aspect. The symbols are a wonderful addition to your spiritual toolbox.

If you are not at Level 2 yet, this chapter should give you some insights and information about the tools. But please realize that intention setting and releasing your conditioning can be done equally effectively through your self-practice. I do believe the symbols help, of course, but that does not mean this stage of spiritual development is only accessible through these sending tools.

Having a clear intention, asking your inner wisdom for guidance, and being alert for what unfolds is available to all of us.

Sending Reiki as a Spiritual Contemplation

I am a huge fan of journaling and always encourage my students to start a journal, as it is very useful to keep track of what you send to. This also builds a useful record should you be inclined to go back and look for patterns in your behaviour later.

In my case, the journal helps me to see subtle progress. Changes often can be slight or even imperceptible, but when you look at your journal entries over a period of six months or so, the shifts can be massive. Being able to discern a pattern of a shift can be encouraging when you get the feeling you are spinning your wheels!

In my journal, each day I start a clean page. I date it at the top, then write a sentence that summarizes what I wish to focus Reiki on that day as clearly as I can. I top it off with a drawn Power symbol to help focus my intention, and then I send Reiki using my customary sending technique.

If you want to try this activity without symbols, you can still write intentions. Of course, affirmations work perfectly fine without symbols. And as you do your own self-Reiki, you can follow the same principles as outlined below.

In my lineage, a Reiki *send* is done for fifteen minutes. During the send, as a rule, I keep a light focus on my *label* (the sentence I wish to focus Reiki on). I try not to allow myself to daydream on a tangent, and when I catch my mind meandering, I gently bring myself back to the label, reread it, and focus on my breath, on my hands, and on sensations in other parts of my body.

You do not want to keep too tight a hold on your mind, as insights and intuitive wisdom often come through during the send. You will miss this if you are overly focused on trying to stop your mind from thinking and settle down—the keyword for this practice is *gentle focus* (not *control freak*). You are holding a delicate intention—a wish, or prayer if you like—and offering it up to the universe. Your intention should be to shine the light of awareness onto the issue.

When we send to an issue, we are laser-focusing Reiki to a specific request. We are committing our time to send healing, and we have written our focus down on paper. From an intention standpoint, this is already bringing a lot of energy to bear on the issue—which signifies that we are saying to ourselves that this is a priority.

On top of this, we are sending healing to this specific issue. Essentially, we are bringing the attention of the universe to bear on our issue—so, how can nothing happen? It's not possible. Sending Reiki *always* works, but it may not work in the way you thought or wanted! And this is what I would like to spend some time on next.

Aligning Your Intention to the Correct Outcome

At this stage of spiritual development, we are harnessing the power of intention, but it is important to understand that what you think you want and what you actually want can be very different things. It can sometimes feel like there are two parts of you operating, a wise you (what some people refer to as a "higher self") and a conditioned you. This is actually quite true as your conditioning can often fool you into believing you really need to follow a certain path, or achieve a certain goal in order to attain happiness, but your wiser self (your lightbulb inner truth) knows that this is not the path to happiness and will tell you this through the body's reactions. It is quite a journey to uncover all the layers of conditioning to see more clearly, and so sending Reiki to issues and intentions will sometimes work wonderfully (when you are aligned with your inner truth) and sometimes not work at all (when you are aligned with your conditioning).

Often people become discouraged when they send to something, and it goes "wrong." For example, you send to the concept of fixing a relationship, and your partner leaves you anyhow, or you send to buying a house you want, and someone swoops in and puts in an offer before you can. On the surface, it appears that Reiki has either made the complete opposite happen, or it has simply failed totally in giving you what you requested.

And herein lies the advantage of hindsight. Having kept a Reiki sending journal for many years, I can see all the misfires; in fact, they became clear to me after only a few years of sending and observing what happened. In all cases where Reiki sending seemed to give me the opposite result to what I wanted, I can see with hindsight the reason for the misfire, and the door that opened because another door closed. "It's not for your higher good" seems such a cliché, but in my experience it really does seem true.

In some cases, the unfolding was simply a matter of time. As well as the question "is it for your higher good?" is also an aspect of timing. Our conditioned egos want everything to happen immediately but an unfolding process needs to take place. With experience, it is easier to accept this reality. We have spent decades piling on layer upon layer of dust, and it often takes some time to clean it all off again.

Timing Is Everything

To take a very simple example, I used to be quite an addicted smoker and had tried many times to quit. When I reached Level 2, I started sending Reiki to quitting smoking; and when this didn't work—I was still giving in to my urges—I started experimenting with sending to different *labels* (wordings), hoping to hit upon a "magic" phrase, and to affirmative statements like "I am free of the desire to smoke," "My lungs are healthy and smoke free," "to harmonise the root cause of my smoking," and the more direct: "I have stopped smoking," "I no longer smoke," and "I am no longer addicted to smoking." On and on this list goes. This took place over the course of about two years!

By this time, I was now teaching Reiki and feeling somewhat strange about hopping out back for a quick smoke at break time. Smoking was not really in my image of what a "good" Reiki master should look like; and yes, I know there was a whole story around that idea too that needed to shatter, but that came later! Eventually, I was becoming quite frustrated at the lack of movement on this issue and my continued addiction, as well as my inability to crack it. Then one fine day, I woke up and stopped. Just like that.

It was the weirdest thing. After years of struggling with this addiction, *poof,* just like that it was done. No cravings, no eating sweets, no coughing up gunk. My other friends who had given up and suffered the usual post-smoking after-effects were amazed and annoyed!

Why was it so easy for me? To this day, I have no idea, but it taught me a very handy lesson: Timing is everything. For whatever reason, the timing of when to give up was not in my control, and ter how much pushing and shoving I did to use my will power and my skills (I also tried hypnotherapy, acupuncture, guided visualization, and other things in addition to Reiki), it was not going to shift until it shifted.

Now, many people would take that statement and see it as permission to just give up all action and keep smoking, and this would be missing the point. I was invested and focused on giving up smoking. I was taking positive action to move towards my goal. As a result, when I had the urge to stop, I followed it wholeheartedly. What I would do differently, if I could, is not so much change the actions I took, but skip the angst I put myself through. This is the thing I urge you to contemplate with me.

If I had known then that it would take two years and I still had to do all the sending, use all the other methods, and just stay focused on the intention that giving up smoking was important to me, that would have been enough. I didn't have to add the self-hatred, the frustration, the thoughts *Why is this taking so long?* and *What is wrong with me?* All the harsh self-talk and bullying I put myself through was totally, utterly pointless, and not helpful from a kindness perspective.

Indulging in angst is something I try to do much less of these days, because now I know that there is a timing element to everything. Things unfold when they unfold, and not a second earlier.

It's Not in Your Best Interest

I really do believe that the universe has a much better way of turning out if I just relax and let things unfold. They unfold anyway, whether I like it or not, but it's a lot more fun and causes a lot less inner angst if I really trust that.

When you send to a job, and you don't get it, change the way you are looking at things to encompass the bigger picture. What is it you are after? That specific job or any job that brings you joy, something you want to be doing, something that wakes you up on Mondays raring to go? Isn't that more like it than one particular job? If you write labels with intentions that point to the very best of what you are looking for, you allow things to unfold in new directions, and with surprising results.

I find if I am holding onto one thing too tightly, then the resulting tension creates nothing but suffering. If I open my mind and remind myself of the bigger picture, different options and avenues open that can be exhilarating to see, and also expand my life enormously.

When you open your mind like this, every sending becomes an adventure. You genuinely don't know what is going to pop up around the corner, and that's the fun of it all. You are curious and enjoying life, eager for what will present itself next.

If I don't get this job, you could think, *what other opportunity is unfolding? Perhaps it's not a job at all? Maybe a collaboration or working for myself or freelancing? Who knows! As long as I'm jumping out of bed eager for the day, who cares!*

Sending Reiki to things you want helps you to gain this type of clarity, spending time with your labels can be enlightening all on its own, what do you want, really? Open your mind and heart to the reason you want this job, this relationship, this house, this direction—what do you think it will give you? Happiness, financial security, acceptance in the eyes of others, what? Sometimes you really can't see it until you begin to send, and then the symbols and Reiki have a way of helping you enlighten to yourself—perhaps during the send itself you will become aware of the underlying motivations surrounding the label you've chosen for the issue, and sometimes you will see it later on, and sometimes you just have to walk headfirst into a lesson to really get it!

When I was working in the corporate world, I was unhappy and I attributed the stress of it all to not having the right job. So I switched from a consumer-side research agency into doing client-side research for a big corporation, as I thought it would be less stressful and more rewarding. I sent Reiki to the "perfect interview" and sent Reiki to "getting the job" —and both happened.

I was intensely focused on my work in those days, not the open-minded type. I can still clearly remember having the gut feeling that this career move was a very bad idea and ignoring it. I was walking down the corridors toward my interview with a feeling of dread in the pit of my stomach.

To be honest, I got caught in a common Reiki trap. Because I sent Reiki to these specific things, and got them, I figured the outcome must be to "my highest good." Well no! I sent Reiki to these specific things and I had a bad feeling in my gut, and *that* was what I should have been paying attention to! The Reiki had worked to inform me of what would be in my best interest.

Anyway, painful story short, I spent six months loathing my new job and got out as quickly as I could. Moral of the story? Listen to myself—especially my body. Other moral of the story? Don't abdicate my responsibility for choices and decisions to some elusive higher power outside myself.

When we send Reiki to ourselves, to issues and the labels we use to define them, we are enlightening ourselves. The response doesn't always come tied in a pretty pink bow, and it isn't handed to us on a silver platter. And sometimes our ego doesn't like the answer. There is an unconscious belief, *If I send to something and it works out, then what I experience next must be for my highest good.* Yes, it *IS*, but it may not be fun.

My six-month torture with a company that was not a good fit for me helped me to clarify what it was I genuinely wanted. Certainly, I knew I was not cut out for big corporate. I knew I didn't play politics well, and I knew I preferred to be autonomous. After this experience, I went on to freelance, and eventually to set up my own company and become my own boss, which is pretty much what I have been doing for the past fifteen years. In hindsight, this was a very clarifying experience for me and served my highest good.

If it feels like I am giving contradictory signals, the nuance here is worth understanding. I took the job thinking it was in my highest good, hated it, and quit. And yes, it was to my highest good, *and* it was painful. Oftentimes, our most powerful lessons are the most painful. I was way out of connection with my own body's messages. I didn't trust myself and so taking this job, learning the lessons of what I didn't want, and starting to align with what brought me joy was all very necessary. Joy versus pain would have been the clue.

Could I have avoided the pain? Of course! I could have listened to my gut. I could have realized sooner that this was not a direction that would bring me joy and strengthen my life force. But when I look back at the mindset I was in at the time of the interview, I can see that nothing was going to change my conditioned mind. My gut was screaming loudly, and it didn't have a chance. For me, at that time, going through the misery of my gut telling me, "I told you so" after the fact, was the only way for me to learn that specific lesson.

Now, when my gut starts screaming, I listen. (Well, most of the time.)

Use Reiki Sending as a Navigational Tool

Every time I send Reiki to something, I learn. I learn what I truly want and what I don't want. The so-called success of a send may turn out to be a failure, and the failure of a send may turn out to be a success. What we term *successes* and *failures* is entirely dependent on the likes and dislikes of our conditioned mind. That is all. When we look back over our lives, it is evident that some of our most stunning so-called failures open doors to the most amazing next opportunities.

As we deepen our self-awareness, an important step in our growth is the loosening up of our ideas about success and failure. These days, I send Reiki to pretty much everything I am stuck with, and find it inspiring what comes out of this small devotion of time and energy. It is part of my daily spiritual practice, and I encourage you to make it part of yours.

As a daily practice, what could you gain more insight around? Like a daily alignment to your inner truth, fifteen minutes is all that a Reiki send takes.

It is also interesting as to how things have evolved as I have journeyed further on my spiritual path. In the beginning, I was sending to specifics, like getting a job or finding a tenant for my flat. I was sending to successful meetings, stopping bad habits. When I look back over the labels that I wrote in my sending journal, they are quite externally focused. It was exciting though to see how things unfolded, as I recall, and to see that I quickly built a trust that one way or another, things would certainly unfold!

As time went by, a much deeper aspect to sending unfolded for me that allowed me to be, essentially, my own therapist. I highly recommend this form of sending.

We can match our sending to our life circumstances. When we hit resistance, we can use Reiki to gently shine a light on it so that we can see more clearly where we are holding on too tightly or trying to control too much. We can use our tools to maximize our growth if we remain alert to what comes up. And when we need some direction or feel we are not sure how to deal with something, we can send to affirmations that will help us to be more prepared and more capable of allowing life fully in.

Sending to Resistance

Sending to life events that you notice make you tense or resistant when you think about them is incredibly supportive and an act of kindness on your part. The easiest and most natural way to do this is merely to be alert for what is coming up inside your body during the day. In the beginning, it may be that things are popping up all the time, there is so much drama and discord in your mind! But rest assured, as you decondition your mind, the discord becomes less hectic and all-consuming. It becomes easier to spot resistance and send to it, so you can move through it more quickly. You really can work with anything right as it comes up. So, be prepared to drill deeply into it, not just to try to push it aside or bury it more deeply in your system.

Disturbing events may be external, but events only cause suffering because of your internal resistance to them. Events are as is. Disturbance is the response in your body.

Simply look at what comes up for you during the day. What little or big tension do you notice? It may be as small as getting stressed because of getting to a meeting late. Looking at the incident, what would you like support with? How would you like it to be different?

You could send Reiki to a label simply stating, "I want to be calm and relaxed when I am running late," or you could dig a little to investigate, using a label such as: "What is the root cause of why I am stressed when I am late for meetings?" You could even problem-solve by sending Reiki to a label like: "Ideas to avoid being late in future."

It doesn't really matter what you send to, as the focused intention of enlightening yourself to anything to do with your stress and resistance is all that is needed here. Your mind will go where it needs to go if you hold it on the same focus with gentle discipline.

As you spend fifteen minutes in quiet contemplation of your intention, pay attention to the Reiki flowing through your hands; is the flow powerful or mild? It's helpful to place your hands on a cushion or other inanimate object to send Reiki to concepts. This is so that you can get a good sense of Reiki flow through the hands without any confusion. If you use your own body, then you are never quite sure if the Reiki is flowing to the concept or to the body part you are touching itself. If the sensation in your hands is relatively quiet, might there be a better intention you could focus on? You probably don't need to write a new label if another phrase comes to mind; pay attention to what your intuition tells you is best and go with that.

Maybe as you contemplate "I want to be calm and relaxed when I am running late" it comes to your attention that you are always stressed because there is never enough time in the day to get all the things you crammed into your appointment book done.

Maybe you realize your tension has nothing to do with being late, that what your spirit is craving is simply "I want to be calm and relaxed." As you contemplate this, perhaps you notice your hands become much hotter and the sensations in your body intensifying, and you notice a deep sadness emerging from your heart and gut. If so, stay with the sadness, notice how much you yearn for this calm peacefulness, and notice what else comes up to support you.

Perhaps you get a sense that you need to drop commitments or ask for more support, or maybe that you could say No more often. Who knows what wisdom comes up from a simple little label? All the richness you need, all the knowledge, it is all within you. Your spirit is so eager to come out and talk to you, even for just fifteen minutes a day.

Sending to Difficult Relationships

If you are hitting discord with a person, I always suggest using a simple label like "perfect resolution of my relationship with X" as a starting point. Be aware of what is coming up as you send Reiki to the label while thinking about this person. Try to stay objective but be honest. What thoughts are coming up? What images or memories? And what emotions do these stir up in you? If you have a history with this person, it may take several Reiki sends to unravel the story, so be patient with yourself.

There is an inbuilt desire in us to get rid of our issues quickly and cleanly, but the truth is often much messier. Relationships are multifaceted and usually take some unravelling. If your relationship issues built over years you can imagine that the layers of discord run deep. The unpicking of a given issue may take years, or it may be extremely quick, who knows? The trick is to keep open and be curious as to what will unfold. Perhaps it will dissolve just like that, and perhaps it will require more picking, more curiosity, more openness.

If we view life more as a journey, we are less likely to get caught up in a quick-fix scheme or in denying a problem even exists. We are more likely to patiently work through issues and obstacles like a detective in an investigation, following leads, coming up to dead-ends, trying other avenues, and always trusting there is an answer to the puzzle and we can find it if we are patient and persistent.

Often the mere act of sending to the intention "to harmonize or resolve my relationship with X" sends a strong signal to the subconscious mind: *I am ready to look at this.* The follow-up of sending Reiki energy to the same intention day after day superpowers it and brings the force of the universe to bear on that issue to support you.

This is not the same as wiping a problem away. It usually means you simply see more clearly what is truly happening as opposed to what you imagined or hoped was happening.

Here's an example. Around the time I gave birth to my first daughter, I moved to a new country. Having landed with no support network and a small baby, and being a new mother, I was clueless. I wanted to give my daughter lots of love and attention, but I literally exhausted myself trying to run the "perfect" home, be the "perfect" wife, and love my child and give her the most attention I could. In my rush towards perfection, I totally neglected myself and spiralled into postpartum depression.

During several difficult months of recovery from depression, I leaned heavily on my own mother, calling her long-distance for advice and support. But in every call, I was coming off as defensive, upset, and angry—the opposite of what I wanted and needed from her. My story was that she was criticizing everything I was saying, that she disagreed with my parenting style, and essentially was telling me I was a bad mother. This was the last thing I needed, and it felt like a disaster in terms of the downturn in our relationship. So I decided to write the label "to the perfect resolution of my relationship with my mother" and send Reiki to it.

I didn't feel much resolve during the sending session itself, but during the very next call I was amazed at the result. My mother had not changed one bit, but I could finally hear what she was saying without my own filter changing the meaning. What she was describing was her own experience, her own way of doing things, and how mothering was done in her day. I had taken all that information and put meaning on top of her words. "I used to do this and that, and it worked" is what she was actually saying, and I heard "I used to do this and that and it worked, so the way you are doing it is wrong, and by the way your mothering decisions suck."

Hah! No wonder I was upset!

I was also not being honest with myself about this notion of perfect mothering that I couldn't live up to, and that's what sending Reiki to the obstacle ultimately helped me to see.

It was bordering on miraculous. Once you see something, it's hard to "unsee" it.

From then on, my conversations with my mother improved immeasurably as I stopped getting so defensive and started to hear what she was saying, rather than the meaning I overlaid on it.

This is another reason why I am such a fan of journaling. When you write down an actual conversation and remove all the emotion and your own filters from it, the reality of what is being said becomes clearer. Our minds have a horrible way of embellishing things in a not-so-nice light.

Sending Reiki helps you to see what is real.

As an addendum, it didn't stop there. I have sent to my relationship with my mother many times over the years, not in the hope that she will change or do something differently, but in the hope I will more clearly see the truth of what is happening, and so gain more clarity over what I embellish and what is actually being said. This work requires a willingness to see what you are doing to yourself, and a desire to stop it and be kinder. It also lets you see the other person more clearly, not as some kind of superhuman but as another human being, just like you, trying her best, just like you.

I have sent to many relationships over the years, and sometimes it has brought me the clarity that, yes, this person is not interacting in a healthy way with me and needs to be let go. This can bring a different kind of clarity, whereby you see how your desire to make things work out creates your suffering, given the reality that the relationship is toxic. In these situations, it's important to see again what you are doing to yourself—hanging on to a toxic relationship is not kind.

Work on surrounding yourself with people who inspire, support, and love you exactly as you are. This will provide you with a huge source of strength and enjoyment. Life really is supporting you.

If we are engaging in toxic patterns, unhealthy relationships, and other behaviours that keep us stuck and we ask for help, then we must be willing to accept the help that comes. Often, we think that sending Reiki to toxic patterns will release us gently and kindly, but this is not always the case. If we are hanging on tightly and not willing to let go on the one hand but sending Reiki and asking to let go on the other hand, then we literally may have to be shaken by life, perhaps violently, to be released.

If this happens, remember what you sent to. What was your request to the universe? Then stay focused on the result you got. Did you get what you asked for?

I have seen this happen in cases where there is a one-sided request or a hidden agenda in operation. For example, Mary will send to the "perfect resolution of her relationship with John" but secretly wants John to stay with her, change his ways, and become her loving Prince Charming. She writes a label and sends to "the perfect resolution," while in honesty, she wants the impossible. When you ask for resolution, you will get it, and maybe for this to happen it's not you and your grasping that can see the light, but him and his clarity that wins through. And maybe John leaves Mary. She gets what she wanted, which is the resolution of an otherwise toxic relationship that was damaging to her and to him. At the moment he leaves her, however, she will probably feel like her world has collapsed, and that sending Reiki has done a very bad thing. With hindsight, she will come to see things differently.

Do bear in mind that when you ask for greater self-awareness, or to have greater peace in your life, that this means you will need to let go of all your toxic and unhealthy habits and patterns of behaviour in order to get peace and insight. You cannot see your inner light if you are not prepared to discard the layers covering it.

Working with Negative Emotions

Emotions like negative self-talk, outbursts of anger, depression, and fear feel unpleasant and are always opportunities for growth. When we try to grow as a result of these types of emotional experiences without first really identifying their root causes, it can be fruitless. Trying to positive-think your way out of negative self-talk may work temporarily out of sheer will power, but in the long term it doesn't give you peace. There will always be a constant power struggle between good cop/bad cop. Essentially such struggles are just one part of your ego's conditioning fighting against another.

Ideally, using Reiki to send to emotions such as these will help to shine a light on the root cause of emotional issues and help you to move through them and learn. Sending to the root cause requires alertness as to what you are requesting. My advice is to work on them in bite-sized pieces—sending to the root cause of *all* your anger or *all* your fear would be a recipe for overwhelm.

Just remember that Reiki sending works and that you are firing off requests that really get answered. Assume if you are struggling with anger issues that the anger is probably deeply rooted with many layers! Imagine you write a label stating you are ready to look at *ALL* of it. And Reiki delivers you what you asked for. All the anger you have stuffed into your system over the decades, from childhood onwards, comes up into your awareness simultaneously. Every single time you have gotten angry and not fully shown it, every single time you have been frustrated by things as mundane as traffic and as significant as betrayal— this is not self-care and will most likely traumatise you even more deeply.

It is kinder to assume that your life is providing you with exactly the right opportunity to look at any issue at exactly the right time. By all means, look at anger. But look at anger as it's tied to a specific issue. If you got angry sitting in traffic and wonder why you cannot just sit in peace, then send Reiki to "the root cause of my anger *when sitting in traffic.*" Right there and then, during this one little incident of anger, all the wisdom exists for your freedom. Overwhelming yourself with all the anger you have ever felt in your life would be counterproductive, whereas homing in on a small incident that is rich in information—now you are getting somewhere!

When I do this for myself, I notice all kinds of things. I am never angry at the traffic (that would be ridiculous!), I am angry at myself for *choosing* this route, I am angry at *not listening to the intuition* that told me to leave earlier, I am angry at *agreeing to meet during rush hour*. So many little thoughts and hints, so rich for data mining! What is going on in that head of mine? What crazy beliefs? What underlying assumptions am I making?

These individual incidents are much easier to define and will give you a better chance to really drill down to your root causes and assumptions than bigger, more layered obstacles. Amazingly, taking care of small things makes a huge impact when it comes to the big things. So, start wherever you are. Your daily life will give you everything you need.

When I am journaling for myself, I am particularly interested in the small incidents that I blow out of proportion. The little moments when I think, *Well, I'm getting a bit worked up over nothing!* Pay attention to the moments during your day when things throw you off-kilter or when you notice your peace has disappeared. There are gems for you to work with at such moments to keep deepening your awareness and becoming more and more awake. Everything that happens during your day, from the minute you wake up onwards, is an opportunity to dust your inner lightbulb. Anything that causes you suffering is an opportunity for healing and harmonizing, and to gain more clarity. Sending is an incredibly effective technique.

When you begin to see your entire life as a spiritual journey, not only the moments you are doing Reiki or are on retreat and sitting on a yoga mat, then every moment is meaningful. Every single moment is an opportunity to see if you are relaxed and joyful or stressed and tense.

As you work through your conditioned algorithms, you naturally become more aware of the light shining within you. As this light begins to make a stronger connection with you, it also shines qualities out into the world that you want to nurture and grow. Qualities are things you deeply value, like love, creativity, independence, connection, or honesty. Using Reiki, we can connect more deeply with our true qualities and live more authentically as a result.

Sending to Affirmations

As a rule, whatever you desire is within your grasp. This may seem a generous claim, but I have found it to be true, although only when applied honestly. Genuine desire as opposed to egoic covetousness comes from our inner truth. Often, the root of a genuine desire for something will always be shrouded under so many layers of conditioned thought and resistance that we misinterpret it.

When I was younger, I used to go to self-improvement workshops focused on getting rich. We would write ludicrous affirmations geared toward making a million dollars in one year or being financially independent within five years, as if affirmations were magical wands to wave about and then sit back and watch cash fall from the sky.

The key to affirmations is to be very honest and specific. Get clear on what you really want—and *why*. Do you want a million dollars? Why? A million dollars is only good if you do something with it, so what is it for? Do you want it so you can *feel secure with it sitting in your bank account?* So you can *quit the job you hate?* So you can *follow your heart's desire?* And what if you could do all that *without* a million dollars?

Affirmations need to be honest to be real. And if we honestly ask for what we want, we can have it. I'm not talking about being honest about wanting a million dollars; I'm talking about being honest about wanting what you think the money (or whatever you say you want) will bring you.

When I was young, I wanted to be happy like the princesses in the fairy tales. I wanted to live happily ever after. And I thought in order to do that I needed a prince. For most of my older teens and early twenties, I was on an obsessive search for my "prince" and was morbidly unhappy when I wasn't in a relationship. This frankly sucked for me, as I was more likely unattached than attached during this time (I can't imagine why). My focus was way off at that point, and because I was confusing happiness with being in a relationship it was not a fun time.

If I had been using affirmations and Reiki during this time, I have no doubt I would have been writing labels like "I have my perfect prince" or "I am married happily ever after." I never questioned what I thought a partner would give me; that only happened years later when I was finally married and realized the folly in trying to make another person responsible for my happiness.

In designing your affirmation labels, be clean and clear. I suggest sticking with qualities or behaviours you value rather than the acquisition of material things or making external changes. Affirmations are written in the present tense. For example, you would say, "I am loving and kind" rather than "I will be loving and kind." They are also written as positive assertions (hence, they are called affirmations), and do not contain words that negate, like never, not, or no.

The act of writing an affirmation can be a clarifying exercise. Often, we are super clear on what we don't want: for example, I don't want my friends to put me down and bully me, I don't want to be stressed at work, and I don't want to be in debt. And taking time to imagine how the opposite of that negative experience will feel—and then putting it into words—can be surprisingly difficult, especially if the thing we dislike, or even hate, is a pattern that has run our lives for a long time. For example, we can get so used to hanging around people that put us down that it can almost be comfortable, and the thought of hanging around people who treat us with respect and love can seem alien and even uncomfortable.

The feelings that come up when you are crafting your affirmation are useful to notice. They should be a stretch, but not too much so. Notice also the negative beliefs that may come up as you begin to design your affirmation. Perhaps you are in a stressful job and would like to have a different job where you feel less stress and more joy, but as you craft your affirmation, you notice you have a belief that "work should be hard" or "work is never fun." This discovery shows you why you took a stressful job in the first place, and what is holding you there. It will also show you the internal struggle you have faced to align with more joyful work because your belief program was running a script of "work should be hard" and life was complying.

Sometimes sending to an affirmation will loosen up our beliefs and sometimes it's helpful also to send Reiki to harmonise the belief program. In other words, sending Reiki to both "I am happy and joyful in my work" *and* "I release the belief that work should be hard."

In the beginning, reach for an affirmation that is a stretch and yet also believable. For example, if your aim is to feel joyful, but you have never felt that way before, it is pointless to try to make the leap in one go. It is much more effective to take a single, small step in that emotional direction. You might affirm, "I am content."

When we send to affirmations, it's important to use the Reiki sending period to contemplate the affirmation we have written. Gently keep focused on the affirmation and allow it to bring up memories or feelings that most closely match it. If you are sending to "I am content," feel all the times this has been true.

Also, pay attention to the self-sabotaging thoughts and memories that may appear. Allow room for all the reasons why you shouldn't or can't be content, and images of all the other things in your life that prevent your contentment to reveal themselves to you. These intrusions show you what resistance remains that needs to be worked on. Therefore affirmations and releasing resistance work hand in hand.

We are moving towards a future we would like to see more of, and also taking care of the resistances that come up to obscure and inhibit the arrival of this future.

Your work with affirmations is likely to evolve over time, as it did for me. In the beginning, you may well be writing labels like "I am a millionaire!" and then noticing what happens. As with any label, you will be gathering information, seeing where your resistance lies, or where any misinterpretation is. But as you work deeper, especially as you come into a deeper understanding of your true nature and the qualities you value, you will continue to revisit the same labels yet to craft them differently. Labels like "I am a millionaire!" evolve into "I am abundant!" and eventually "I am abundance!"

Remember, every label or affirmation you send Reiki to is part of the process of your personal evolution, so never wrong. As with anything in Reiki, you cannot go down a wrong path. The path is always supporting you in peeling off layer after layer of mental debris, and with each new layer gone bringing you closer to alignment with your inner truth.

Working on Ourselves, Not Others

Often during label work we are tempted to help others, especially if we have seen the positive effects of this technique at work in our own lives. I always caution against this. If you want to help others then send them Reiki or give them a hands-on treatment. Better still, encourage them to study Reiki themselves and begin their own self-healing journey. If you're a Level 3/Master, go ahead and give them an attunement. But it's best not to try to fix other people's lives by sending to labels on their behalf. When we are doing our own inner work, I hope it is becoming clear that our own courage and readiness is key to receiving the insights. Your friends and loved ones (or whomever you desire to help) may not be ready yet, so you won't be doing them a favour.

Essentially, with sending to labels and affirmations we are using Reiki as a clarifying tool; laser-focusing on a single issue with the help of Reiki, we hope to come to see things differently—more clearly, more realistically, and more honestly—and this is what shifts things for us. But the same clarity can sometimes bring unexpected results, and these results may not always be interpreted by others as positive.

A phenomenon I have seen several times related to misguided sending is when we try to help friends by sending to the resolution of their relationships with spouses and partners. Your sends can have disastrous results if the loved one decides to leave. Of course, whatever outcome occurs is for the highest good of the relationship. With the departure is a sign that with more clarity and harmony, the dysfunction has been seen by that person, which is why he or she chooses to leave.

But what happens to your own relationship with your friend if it is perceived that you instigated the departure? In the cases where good-hearted students have tried to help their friends, it has often resulted in the termination of a friendship, or at the very least, a tension that could not be easily resolved.

Meddling in other people's affairs is never a good idea. Instead, work on your own issues. And if you need everything to be OK for everyone else before you can be happy, then well done, you have identified your first issue to work on!

Take care when writing labels that you are writing them for yourself. A label stating "I want Margaret to treat me kindly" or sending Reiki "to get my son to do all his homework on time" are clearly issues that have nothing to do with you. As a parent or a partner you may feel you have a right to demand a change in someone else's behaviour, but the labels you originally ascribed to Margaret should be "I want to treat myself with kindness." Frankly, this includes how you allow Margaret to treat you, as people treat us unkindly only if we are around to take the abuse. If you are dedicated to treating yourself with kindness, it's obvious what you should do with people who are unkind to you.

The same goes for our children and their lives. They will push every button possible to wake us up! Can you see whom you are really mad at? If Mark's behaviour is bugging you, how about sending to "getting all my work done on time"? You could also send to "why it is so important to me that Mark does all his homework." This would facilitate some discoveries.

Start to become more aware of how you are trying to make everyone else conform to your belief structures, be willing to look at what your belief structures are if you're uncertain, and then decide if they're still relevant and worth keeping.

Clearing the Path

The second stage of the Reiki path is all about seeing our mental conditioning and algorithms and cleaning them up. It is magical how issues can dissolve, relationships can improve, and even success can begin to come our way as we become less reactive and more open to what life has to offer. But there is a learning curve with being skilful at sending, and for many labels, we will be disappointed when things don't go our way.

What your conditioned ego wants and what your inner light wants is not quite the same thing. With experience, and trust, you will begin to see that when you send out a request through Reiki sending, it is always bringing you into deeper connection with who you really are.

As we master this stage, we notice that everything in life feels looser and easier. Life continues as normal, but with much less angst and stress. Things bother us much less. We have greater contentment and acceptance. We are still in a stage of spiritual development where we are living in a relative world—perceiving ourselves and Reiki as separate entities. Most people will stop here because life is better, and when it's not, there is Reiki to fall back on. There has been a significant improvement in the quality of life, and the tools are great for life management going forwards.

If this is where you stop, then great, your life is easier and you are happier, and that makes the journey thus far worthwhile. Keep using your tools and doing daily self-treatment and Reiki sends. That will be a positive, grounding experience.

However, you are only halfway. I would encourage you to take a leap of faith and jump into the abyss with me. In the next stages of Reiki practice, we encounter the paradoxical truth of Reiki. Internally, we enter the space of our truth, which is the only place we will find lasting and eternal freedom.

8.
Minding the Gap

*Enlightenment is always there.
Small enlightenment will bring great
enlightenment. If you breathe in
and are aware that you are alive—
that you can touch the miracle of
being alive—then that is a kind of
enlightenment.*

—Thich Nhat Hạnh

In this book, the main assumption we are working with is that the freedom and happiness you seek is available right inside you, right this moment. Our egoic conditioning will have us believe that our happiness is found outside in the world of achievement or attainment and is always looking into the future or into the past to try to find the next thing to work on. But our freedom is found in the present moment; this is when we can discover everything we need for our happiness is right here, right now.

But to get to the heart of our assumption we need to make a paradigm shift, and this is not a shift we can make through our thinking—it can only be done when we stop thinking and *see the truth of who we are*. This is, unfortunately, where words will fail us, as *words form concepts and thoughts, and right here, right now is not a concept or a thought. It's an experience.*

The only way to understand what I am pointing to is to experience it for yourself, which is why I keep directing you to your own experience as the only doorway into your truth. Another way to describe your inner truth, one that I have previously referred to as the "big bright light," is that this is the truth that exists within you beneath all the layers of your egoic conditioning.

But even these terms set the ego off on a search for a "big bright light" or my "true self" as if these are objects to be found rather than actual experiences to be had. If I can put it in very simplistic terms, let me give an example of walking my dog. When I am walking the dog and have a friend with me (or I am on the phone) my attention is obviously moving in an outwards direction, toward my friend and the conversation we are having. I am paying minimal attention to my surroundings or my dog. The walk, in this case, is a means to an end: to let the dog do her business. My friend is a welcome distraction from my chore. You could see this as an analogy for the typical attention of most humans: They have a constant outwardly focused and goal-driven orientation. In your own life, you could replace the walk with "work" or "housework," and you'd see what I mean. We typically do chores because we have to, and we welcome distractions of any kind.

The beginning of our spiritual journey is when we realise that if we turn our attention inwards, we can use the walk (or housework, and so on) as a way of getting more in touch with our inner life. Rather than looking for distractions, I begin to use my walk as a meditation, I look inwards and discover a whole new world rich with information. However, the walk is still a means to an end, but now there is a more meaningful reason: I am walking my dog as a chore and also as a personal growth tool. This in itself is a great step forward, as it brings much more meaning to the chore, and I look forward to the walk. Now, the chore itself is not as bothersome as it used to be.

And for most of us, we stop here. Our spiritual journey is one of finding personal meaning in all we do, an opportunity to discover our egoic conditioning and release our contracted thoughts so that our life becomes more and more pleasant.

But what if there was a possibility to walk the dog as the meaning itself, for the simple pleasure and curiosity of seeing what happens in the moment, with no thoughts, no meditation, and no ulterior motive to be doing it. Perhaps you already walk your dog like this, for the pure joy of getting out into nature, seeing what pops out of the bushes, smelling the air, moving your body. If you do, you know what I am talking about. The chore is done joyfully, it's great fun, and you are totally in the moment, enjoying life.

Now, extend that to all aspects of your life: Can you imagine the joy your life would become if all of it were conducted in a similar manner?

This is the next stage of our spiritual journey, to recognise that part of you that is joyfully walking the dog, the part of you that doesn't need a friend or your inner ego narrative for distraction. The part of you that is totally, fully immersed in the walk itself. This is your true self. If you take yourself out for a walk you will soon understand how elusive seeing this part of you can be. You may be breathing the air and then your narrative will state, "Oh, that's so fresh!" and in that moment you have placed a film of separation between you and the air you breathe. You may find yourself immersed in the vibrancy of a flower and almost immediately your mind will state, "Oh! What a beautiful flower!" and so it goes, for the entire walk! When you first notice what you are doing it can be shocking, your entire experience of life is taking place behind this constant narrative in your head.

The importance of realising this cannot be understated. You cannot experience life fully through a story, it is like experiencing eating a strawberry through your description of a strawberry—not the direct, unfiltered experience of eating the fruit itself. This film of separation stops you from directly experiencing your true nature, the thinking covers over the experience and covers over your inner light, it's like you are watching a narrated movie about your life.

If you can catch yourself doing this, congratulate yourself! This simple awareness is all that is needed to bring your attention more and more into the gaps before thoughts hijack your experience.

Spacious Awareness

As we embrace the Reiki spiritual path, we continue to connect with our body, and clear the cache of our conditioned mind. We begin to see more clearly that the conditioning doesn't genuinely define us. Luckily, you do not need to get rid of all your conditioning in order to see your truth, you just need to relax your mind's constant chatter for long enough to notice the awareness in between.

When I do my Reiki, and when I Reiki other people, there is a distinct merging that occurs, and a feeling of timelessness, flow, and total peace within the moment. When my thoughts quiet into nothing, I still exist, I am still aware that I am here. When I am totally in the moment, there is never a problem with anything I am experiencing. The problems only begin again when my mind starts its tyrannical thinking.

Are we simply the jumble of thoughts, sensations, emotional conditions, and programmed beliefs that have formed our experience since childhood? Or are we something more eternal, more infinite, more aware?

Where does your consciousness come from?

This is not a philosophical debate. I am suggesting you engage in self-investigation.

If you have been following the Reiki path for some time, you will be very familiar with the feeling of merging with something bigger than your body. Bring your focus to those moments of merging that you naturally experience during a Reiki sending or self-healing. Relax into the experience and become aware of what is happening. Then observe.

When you drop thought, do you still exist?

When you drop doing anything, just sitting with the send, or just lying with your hands on your body, can you sense the awareness all around you, in you, as you?

Is this not more you than the jumble of thoughts? Does it not feel more real and more alive?

What is this essence that is conscious? What is this essence that is aware it is thinking or looking, or hearing, or feeling? It feels like you, doesn't it? But a bigger, calmer, happier, and freer you.

Deepening into this enquiry is what this stage of spiritual development is all about. As soon as you perceive that you are more than the jumble of conditioned thoughts that you previously called your ego, then the paradigm shift is possible.

If you have been doing Reiki on yourself for years, you will recognize that it has always been there since you did your first self-healing exercise—that moment when you first gave yourself a treatment and sank into the bliss of total relaxation. That exact moment which you have recreated time and time again. This is your true nature, your true self—relaxed, content, totally fine, eternal, awake, and aware. This is where you focus your attention.

Your true self is the part of you that has always been looking out of your eyes from the first moment you can remember. It is the awareness that opens its eyes in the morning, closes them at night, and all the observations in between. Look for yourself. So much of your body, your emotions, your thoughts has changed over the years, but what is aware, what is looking out of your eyes, hasn't this stayed the same? It is eternal and has not changed one bit, wouldn't you agree?

This awareness or presence is the eternal essence many of us are searching for, yearning for. And yet here it is, every morning you wake up. Here it is! The issue we have, and why we search, is the film of separation we have placed around this part of ourselves through our thinking, our constant narrative, and conditioned beliefs.

Doorways into Our True Self

At this stage, I advocate using the Reiki attunements as a spiritual hammer. Every attunement puts a small crack in the structure of our egoic conditioning. If we see our true self as our inner essence, that which is joyfully experiencing life, and our egoic conditioning as the layers covering over this direct experience and separating us from it, we can view attunements as waves of resonance able to penetrate all our layers and vibrate with our essence.

Every attunement brings you the recognition that you are life force, though in the beginning, this may not be a conscious recognition. It could take you thousands of attunements to break the egoic structure wide open, but you can trust that every attunement makes a difference.

Another way of looking at it is that every attunement steps you in and out of universal source energy, and the more times you immerse yourself in pure Reiki energy, the easier it is to become aware when you are "in" and when you are "out."

In means you are experiencing life as your true self.

Out means you are experiencing life through the lens of your ego-conditioned mind.

For example, when I first started practising Reiki, I noticed that I was stressed all the time, except for the one blissful hour each day during which I was doing my Reiki self-treatment. Then I would be relaxed and at peace. In the beginning, I thought Reiki was doing that for me, so in a way, my stress had become the norm. As the years went by, I noticed more and more peace, and less and less stress, until peace became more prevalent than stress. Once the balance shifted and my perspective was healthier, there was a stark contrast when my body became stressed or I experienced mental and emotional turmoil.

Doing regular attunements accelerates this shift in perception, as it steps you fully into the morphic field of universal life force. It seems logical that the more you step in and acquaint yourself to this resonance, the easier it is to see when you are out of resonance and caught by your egoic conditioning.

However, it's useful to understand that this acceleration in insight can also seem more painful now! Whereas in the past I was so used to stress that I could live in it all day long, now I find it intolerable to be stressed for more than a few hours! It seems that as my immersion into my true nature has grown, my tolerance for being in my egoic conditioning has diminished. In that sense, as we deepen into ourselves, we become more curious about what is left to clean up and clearer as to what the actual cause of our stress is in the first place.

We ourselves are in control of the speed of awareness. Full speed ahead is created through daily attunements, or maybe even dozens daily, if we are teaching at maximum capacity. But we always have a choice in our practice. There is no point trying to force your evolution beyond your capacity as you will just deflect, deny, or shut down.

If you are working with trauma, you run the risk of retraumatising yourself if you push your evolution to accelerate. Trying to move quickly and impatiently through resistance is simply showing you your resistance to the resistance! Having the wisdom to know when you are ready for more is really part of discovering your inner balance.

When we start a daily self-attunement practice as a way of merging consistently and regularly with life force and our true self, things tend to get rather interesting. You begin to bump up against all the things, situations, and relationships that are still out of alignment with your inner truth. It generally comes as a shock to people how much unfinished business still exists. Sometimes you may even feel like you are peddling backwards. But this is never the case. All that is happening at this stage is that you are having the recognition that you have deeper layers to let go of.

Remembering your tools is very helpful as you become aware of deeper issues, utilising your self-treatment and sending tools as you keep alert for what seems to be in and out of a more authentic experience of life. Remember also that egoic conditioning takes time to unravel. You will still get caught in dramas, you will still get angry, and you will still react to things. But the conscious recognition that you have a choice as to where you place your attention is a game changer! When that lands solidly in your awareness, you will recognize that what you experience with Reiki is, in fact, the source of your life force, and the outside world and all your opinions about it are simply manifestations coming from the very same source. Everything is one thing.

That's about when you will recognize that your true nature includes all your personality traits, conditions, hang-ups, phobias, and dysfunction as well. You are your whole personality, and much more. Once you develop deep acceptance of your humanity and see that your thoughts are a perfectly normal and welcome part of your human experience, it transforms everything.

Everything Is Welcome

When you start to hold all your thoughts in a much lighter way and stop contracting around them, you will experience a measure of peace and freedom that is a huge relief.

Your opinions are just your conditioning. Take the time to really see this for yourself. Any thought that comes to you—just start to notice. Some pop up and you agree. Some pop up and you disagree. Some pop up and you're not sure. *Do I agree or not?* It is suggested that we have tens of thousands of thoughts a day! We don't filter the activity consciously; we do it unconsciously. And what sticks to the "thought net" to be presented to the conscious mind is just a curated selection. And who's the curator? The filtering is purely done by conditioning.

As I said earlier in the book, the mental filter is like a Google algorithm because it's based on what we've liked before, what we've disliked before, what has an emotional charge to it, what our parents told us was true, what we read in the papers yesterday, and on and on and on. We have little idea of what is in the filters, as they've been building for decades! But one thing is for sure: The filters are not an indication of our inner truth.

What is most shocking about our mental conditioning is the amount of suffering these thoughts produce. But thoughts are so transitory. I'm sure you've had this experience before: You've been very upset by something, and then you do your Reiki, you spend some time on yourself with the intention to balance or heal or release, and you feel much better afterwards. You may credit Reiki with this, but the truth is that you simply dropped the thinking process. You let it go.

And, of course, there are other times when you don't let the thinking go, and you learn something about your attachments. This is the ongoing journey to bring all parts of your conditioning into the light.

As you focus more of your attention in the gaps in between or underneath your thinking, into the essence of who you are, what you will notice is that all problems become less impactful. The drama of thought will grab you and take you on a merry dance, but you now know it's a dance, and know it's not real. And that takes the edge off.

For example, I was having a conversation with another Reiki teacher and she was very upset about something a mutual friend, a peer of ours, was doing. It upset her because it was not the way she felt Reiki should be taught, and she was so upset that she was reacting to the situation with anger, frustration, lots of thoughts, and stress. Yet she also knew it was none of her business and she couldn't do anything about it. She was just stewing in the juices of her own suffering. Recognise this?

There is a very real alternative, and that is to see very clearly, *I have an opinion, and so does this other teacher, and both are correct.* That's the way I saw it when this teacher was speaking to me about it. On the phone she sounded angry as she was saying, "This teacher is doing this and that, she shouldn't be doing this, it's not in the right, authentic nature of Reiki, blah blah." I totally agreed with her, I also had an opinion, but where she and I diverged is that I didn't think my opinion was *right*. In that way, I didn't have to suffer or get angry because someone else was doing something different.

I have plenty of opinions, as I'm sure you can tell from reading this book, and they are useful tools to help me navigate life. In general, my opinions match my life experience, so they give me orientation. In my opinion, for example, it's good to get up and brush my teeth in the morning, make my bed, do some planning for the day. There is a useful and functional aspect of thinking and having opinions. It would actually be a bit disastrous for me to eliminate all my conditioning and only operate out of my inner essence with no structure or frame of reference. I would imagine I would go out to walk my dog and never be seen again! My joyful inner essence would be so immersed in a beautiful flower it would stay staring at it for the rest of eternity!

What we begin to see as we come into a more deliberate connection with our true self is that everything is welcome. We have an essence that is peering out of our eyes and taking in everything it sees, and there is an egoic conditioning that is enabling the essence to function. The problems only arise when we mistake ourselves for the conditioning.

The Paradox of Freedom

When I talk about freedom, it is not the kind that ego thinks of. An ego's perspective of freedom is *I will be free to have only good things come into my life, and I will be free to do whatever I want and not have any bad things happen.* Freedom, to the ego, is a blissful, pain-free, super-successful existence, the big prize at the end of all that darned Reiki!

The real freedom I speak of, by contrast, is the freedom of total acceptance of all parts of yourself. There is a love that emerges for your humanness the longer you stay true to this path. The essence that peers out of your eyes loves life and recognises the essence peering out of everyone else's eyes. It loves the body it is in. It loves the mind with its tricky thoughts, and it loves the ego. It loves the magic of life and the mundaneness. Just being alive is an incredible thing.

The freedom I speak of is living with no attachment or resistance to what you are seeing—there is just love and acceptance for everything exactly as it is. From this perspective, when you stop trying to push and shove your life into all the *shoulds* and *shouldn'ts* you begin to see the ease and grace in everything. Everything moves in a rhythm and flow, and it is truly enjoyable—even when it's not.

An example of this is finding the gift in an illness. Time and time again, I have had amazing, courageous clients work through cancer, disability, depression, physical and emotional pain, and begin to see the gift that the challenge is presenting them. They have a genuine willingness to embrace the situation. With this embracing comes a release of much of the suffering brought on by the thinking about the illness, and clarity about what needs to be done next.

This is the paradox. When we stop the "war on cancer" and stop "fighting the battle," and instead of resisting our situation actually embrace whatever it is, plenty of inspiration, support, and energy comes to meet us and help us respond in much healthier, more productive ways. It doesn't at all mean we stop the conventional treatment or taking our doctor's advice, but we do so with much more clarity and less fear—and this approach often helps us heal in other, sometimes surprising ways.

The freedom we are all so desperately seeking is actually the freedom from believing our ego conditioning, which tells us, *This is right, this is wrong*, as it compares and contrasts every single little thing that we do against everything else.

If you think back to the walking the dog story, it is the difference between walking my dog with my head full of problems, trying to work out solutions, spinning stories of *he said, she said*. You have probably had many walks like this, as have I. This is basically the story of our lives, we sleepwalk through our lives missing all the flowers, the smell of the air, the colours of the trees. When you truly see life as it is, not in your thoughts but firmly in the present moment, it is like walking in the woods and being fully alive to each and every moment. These walks are the ones we remember, they are the awesome ones.

Making every walk an awesome one is the aim of this stage of spiritual growth. It requires a further releasing of old algorithms, but more importantly it requires a consistent and regular focus on what is under all the conditioning. It is the ongoing inner enquiry: *What is this inner light bulb or life force?*

Life Loves Living Life

I used to have a fear that if I surrendered to the gaps in between my thinking—in other words, if I stopped being bullied by the tyrannical thinking—I would become a big blancmange sitting on the sofa watching TV all day. I had this idea that it would be like walking my dog and becoming mesmerised by a flower, not knowing it was time to go home and cook dinner, not being motivated to do anything at all. This is another clever trick of the ego, to assure you that you need its tyranny in order to function.

What I was missing was the crucial discernment of a healthy functioning ego that would tell me, *Stop looking at the flower dear, time to go home and cook dinner.* Instead I had a tyrannical ego that said, *OY! Wake up, dopey, dinner isn't going to cook itself! Look at you, you can't even keep time, you can't even look after your family, you are useless!*

Hopefully your ego isn't that nasty, but in some of the stories we tell ourselves about ourselves, it probably comes close. The unhelpful part of our ego conditioning is what we are working to clear, not the healthy, useful functioning part.

What I have noticed about the gaps in between my thinking is its curious alertness. In moments when I can look at a flower with full awareness, I notice an almost childlike exuberance, I am literally struck with awe. In fact I would suggest that anytime you feel awestruck you are probably in full awareness, as your true self. If you contemplate when these instances occur, you may find your list including a wonderful sunset, the view from a mountain, but other moments when we are fully engaged in life and not the thoughts in our head may include watching your child in a school play, cuddling a puppy, watching a gripping movie. We are often engaged in life, our true self is often operating, and this is an acknowledgement that is helpful in our ongoing journey. We are not looking for some unknown quality, our true self has always been operational, and we've been connected to it many, many times.

Our true self is curious and engaged. It wants to know itself. This is the deep spiritual yearning that brought you to Reiki in the first place, and when you let go of more and more of your conditioned thoughts and beliefs, your true self will become more unencumbered and more expressive. You will be rewarded with creativity, energy, vitality, and a passion for life and living you may never have dreamed possible.

Life bursts through you, you bring your attention to it, and you work on seeing through the egoic tyranny to clear the way for more life. Once you start to see the system at work, it's likely that you will double your efforts to free yourself.

This is the paradox also. Once your ego begins to loosen its conditioned hold, your inner light becomes more of a focus and you begin to see the advantage of more surrender. Even though you begin to see that all are of equal value (to keep your conditioning or to release it), you choose to free yourself and not get stuck in a condition once again. Once you taste the freedom of being unconditioned, you desire to stay in awareness more than you desire the drama.

This is when you will notice you begin to use the Reiki tools much more consciously and conscientiously. The objective is to release yourself from the hook that takes your attention away from your truth and into the condition. Any progress is measured in terms of how much easier it is to come back into your centre, your true nature.

Choose Your Focal Point

There is a conscious choice you must make to develop spiritually. You can consciously choose to contemplate what lies underneath the layers of thought or you can plunge headlong into the drama of life and your thoughts will take you a merry ride. This is the free will we have: where we put our attention. The more we place our attention and intention on our inner essence, the easier it is to stay true to it.

But watch how you get pulled out into the drama time and time again. You can see this just in a simple fifteen-minute Reiki sending. Let's say you begin, tune in to the symbols, relax quickly into your state of awareness, feel merged with all, and then *bam!* A juicy thought comes along and off you go! Then you realize what's happening and drop the thought, and then *bam!* Another one, then drop, and relax, *bam!* And so it goes for the entire fifteen minutes. And this is what you are dealing with at all hours of the day.

Thoughts are bewitching, and the energy you get from drama is strong, so it may even feel good for a while to be dramatic, and then, as it settles, you realize you are exhausted, and the energy doesn't feel that great after all. When you reflect honestly, you realize it takes much more energy to provoke and follow thoughts than you gain from the experience.

Releasing ourselves fully and completely from our conditioning is an ongoing, often lengthy stage of development for most of us. Realizing that our conditioning will always want to pull us back into drama and constriction may feel frustrating, but it is also a source of motivation to keep going. It gets easier. We catch ourselves earlier, and most importantly, we experience more joy and presence in life, which helps keep us motivated.

Coming into full alignment with our life force may also nudge you to realise that once we have enough looseness around our belief structures it is simply a matter of focus. I can direct attention to my thoughts which will spiral this way or that, or I turn my attention to my breath, to my immediate surroundings, or to my task at hand. Sometimes that is all that is needed, I turn my attention to what

I value. Do I value my desire to control? Or do I value where life wants to take me?

Now, the final piece of the puzzle begins to emerge, the feeling that this true nature in us is in fact life itself. The mystery in me is the same as the mystery in you. But the expression of this mystery is what is different. My life and my expression of life is obviously going to be very different from yours, yet we come from the same source. Isn't that amazing?

For example, we may mistake abundance for money, joy for happiness, enthusiasm for productivity, passion for sex, bliss for fleeting enjoyment, gratitude for fear of loss, heart-centred energy for thought-centred energy. These misinterpretations make our life experiences small, fear-based, and grasping.

We are swimming in limitless abundance, it is flowing out of us unconditionally, and when we mistake this abundance and only relate it to money, we begin to tighten around it, trying to keep it, make more of it, spend it wisely. Whatever our conditions are around money, whatever we have been told about money will reflect in what we do with it once we have it, we narrow our field of experience, and in so doing we constrict.

I don't have to tell you this, you can feel it in your own body. If we were to tune in to this impulse of abundance, feel the quality of it, feel into how unconditioned it is, flowing freely and constantly out of us, we would approach things very differently. Instead of grasping to get what we can, we would open our arms and give freely, and receive freely. It would be a balanced and equal exchange of energy. It would become more aligned with the truth of abundance.

The same is true for joy and bliss, it is limitless and always present, yet we search for it in experiences and rewards, and so there is always a fear that it will be taken away, we hang on to our happiness scared the very next person, or thought, will strip us of it. In life, we come across people who are unkind, and we hit situations that challenge us, but when we are centred in the joy and bliss of existence, it doesn't bring suffering. Heart-centred energy is expansive, abundant, passionate, enthusiastic, and creative. But that exact same impulse, when filtered through the conditioned mind, becomes distorted with whatever personal fears we have and ends up expressing itself in a much more fearful, small, and contracted way. We may still experience success, but it comes out as achievement or productivity, which adds stress, takes up energy, and is usually bathed in a fearful undercurrent of trying to protect it all from loss.

This chapter is an exploration of this life force. How does life want to express out of you? What kind of dance are you? Getting acquainted with the impulse is key to our joy and abundance. When we mistake it as a lack and grab for the nearest thing to try to stop it, we miss a huge opportunity. We play small, we stuff ourselves with things rather than exploring what really wants to shine forth. When you begin to look at this impulse as something that wants you to dance to your full potential, the most amazing openness, excitement, and passion begin to fill you and your life. And this is what we explore in this last stage, the idea that life wants to dance out of you in exuberant bigness. It is a big, bright light.

What Is Life's Purpose?

I call this bigness your *life purpose*, but I am aware that the term is fraught with misunderstanding. In truth, your life purpose is to connect and flow with this creative impulse. Most of us will do that in a very small, misunderstood way, and that is understandable—we are following the impulse as an interpretation and doing the best we can. If you are resonating with what I am saying, then you will be pleased to learn that there is another way, which could result in a far bigger experience and enjoyment of life.

When your life purpose shines through, it comes from life itself and has true meaning. It is not made up by the ego or grasped as an outside goal. When the ego sets goals and purpose, it comes from a place of lacking something or trying to gain something and there is a subtle agenda running that whatever is being experienced in this present moment is "not enough." There is a belief *If I can live my life purpose, I will be happy*. But this comes with the assumption, *Unless I find it, I will be unhappy*. When you abide in your true self, you will see life's purpose bursting out of you, and there is nothing much you can do about it. It is not planned or thought out, but more often a movement or impulse that you follow (or not). When you follow it, you usually don't have any clear idea of where you will end up, you just start trusting yourself and the way you feel.

Three years before I moved from Singapore to England, I already knew the move was coming. I could feel the impulse, and in this case, it had a clear direction: I was leaving. I had no idea why or how or when; I just knew it was coming. The usefulness of sensing into the direction your life is taking is that you can start to move with it.

I decided not to renew the lease on my Reiki Centre and instead moved all my classes into a bigger wellness centre to give myself more flexibility. At the time, most people couldn't understand what on earth I was doing, and to be honest, I didn't understand it fully myself; it was simply preparation. Things went along like this for a year, and I wondered if perhaps I had misinterpreted the impulse. And then my daughter, who was struggling academically, was diagnosed with specific learning difficulties. Try as we might to find a good solution in Singapore, it ended up being that the best thing for her wellness and success was to move to the United Kingdom where there was much more scope for her talents as an artist and actor. Out of nowhere, the reason for the move appeared, and I was ready. I had spent two years focused on training Reiki teachers, and it felt to me that I was leaving the Singapore Reiki community in very good shape for its continued success.

This story highlights the qualities of an authentic life purpose rather than the egoic one. In my mind, I could have had a very different purpose, and I could have interpreted the impulse to move a thousand different ways. The impulse when it came up was much more complex than I am describing in a few paragraphs. In the beginning, it felt like my centre was becoming a burden to run and manage, so I had questions: *Maybe I should give it up and move into a bigger space that is managed by someone else so I can focus on my teaching?*

Around the same time, I began graduating many more Reiki teachers. I had the thought that I needed to stop mothering them so much and give them more independence. As all these smaller pushes and prods were unfolding, I noticed a bigger picture of releasing and was curious as to why I was releasing so much of my business. I had the feeling I was preparing for a shift, so when it came, I wasn't caught off guard.

I could easily imagine it as going the other way, of resisting the impulse and trying to hang on to my business, my teachers, my centre, my home. Imagine the mess and the suffering. Imagine my daughter's burden to have to carry all my disappointment as we moved to a new country for her education?

Going with life's impulse, being open to what is being offered is so much easier!

We must have an element of trust and faith. In my case, I could feel where life was taking me, but I had no clarity around why, when, or how. I followed the impulse because I could feel its direction and trusted life enough to follow it. There was an element of the unknown—life impulse takes us into new territory that we wouldn't plan for ourselves, and in that way, it is richer and more expansive than trying to control it is.

And finally, it is 100 per cent supportive. Life comes up to meet you when you move with it. That's not to say it wasn't incredibly challenging to uproot myself and my family and move halfway around the world, but as I had been preparing for three years to do so, it all happened with considerable grace and flow.

Other things unfolded that I would never have planned for, opportunities to release many old patterns of behaviour, as well as a lot of material junk stored in our home! It seemed that the move also allowed for growth in so many other ways, including sowing the seed of this book.

When we arrived in the United Kingdom, there was almost a magical quality to the way the country embraced us and gave us a beautiful home and settled us in. Now my daughter is flourishing, and I have found time to write. The countryside is nurturing in ways I didn't imagine it would be, and I found many opportunities to deepen my own spiritual journey.

As you meet life, it unfolds to the next thing, and then the next thing. Your life purpose is to meet life and bring these creative impulses into manifestation. Our entire human existence allows for manifestation. Life inspires creativity, and we can build, invent, develop, express, experiment. It is miraculous, beautiful, and awe-inspiring.

Life Purpose or Ego Agenda?

When I first started my Reiki master training, it was to get me out of the grind of corporate life. I hated wearing suits, going to meetings, and earning a salary doing something that didn't feel meaningful to me. I had a huge personal agenda. Despite having found my life purpose in Reiki, I didn't recognize this for years. The impulse sparked, but the ego took it and turned it only into a means to free me from corporate life. This is what I mean when I say the impulse is often misinterpreted.

Most people, when they finally recognize their life purpose, are surprised that they are usually more or less on the right track—and have been all along.

I loved teaching Reiki, but in the beginning, I couldn't teach it cleanly, without an ego agenda. I wanted to be free, and I thought teaching Reiki full time would do the job. But I wanted something from Reiki. I struggled for years to make money through my Reiki teaching, and with hindsight, it is no wonder. If you are trying to do something as a means of getting something for yourself, you are always going to struggle. If you are trying to do anything with a personal agenda, it is somehow tainted and cloudy.

Even if you have already found your life purpose, don't expect things to not ever become cloudy. Our conditioning filters everything. Ironically, my success in Reiki came when I went back to my career. I went back into the corporate world because I was fed up with having no money, and then I started offering Reiki classes over the weekend. My financial neediness evaporated, as I was now secure in a job. I no longer felt I needed Reiki to be successful, it was something I offered simply because I wanted to, with no agenda. I offered it cleanly then, as a service, and as something I loved to share. From this perspective, my Reiki practice grew—and it was a very powerful lesson for me.

I come across many teachers who tell me they are not teaching with an agenda but teaching "for the greater good." This equally is an agenda. Thinking of yourself as some kind of saviour of the human race because "other people need" you, in fact, is an agenda of needing to be needed. Being of service can also be an agenda. Serving others only makes sense when that is what life itself demands of you, not as something your ego uses to make itself feel superior.

If you are struggling with your business or your work, it is important to look at your motivations and be honest about the amount of personal work you still must do. Be sincerely working on yourself, stretching yourself to clarify who and what you are. Courageously looking at the beliefs that no longer serve you and doing your utmost to release your agendas is appropriate no matter how advanced you are as a practitioner or teacher.

If you see life purpose as something you set for yourself that comes from your thoughts or your ego, then, by definition, it will have an agenda. Reaching for a goal, grasping for meaning in your life, is a sign you're heading in the wrong direction. Your impulse is within you, and all that is required is for you to pay attention. When you are doing activities that bring you joy, when you are feeling content, fulfilled, and aligned with life, these are the activities which are in keeping with your life purpose.

If you do not have life force impulse bursting out of you and pointing you in a clear direction, or if you are squandering this impulse through misguided grasping for material objects, goals, or relationships, then you still need to spend time doing more inner work in order to keep clearing the way for life's impulse to show you its direction. This creative process is always within you. This impulse is always available. But if your mind is still clouded by a lot of conditioning, you will not interpret it accurately.

Following the impulse is not for personal gain, world recognition, or material success. Maybe that comes, and maybe it doesn't. Following the impulse is about living your life fully. The ego doesn't gain from this—it's not even involved. Even though we are all life force, we each have a unique way of expressing it. For some of us, the life impulse is a huge torrential river cutting a valley through a mountain range, for others it is a meandering brook in pleasant countryside. Trying to force your life to follow a path it doesn't want to follow is an egoic agenda.

To highlight this, let me tell a story.

I met a musician who had been on a spiritual path for many years and had an awakening experience where he gained great clarity on his true nature. He felt his life purpose was to write and sing uplifting songs, which he then spent his savings to professionally record an album. When he released the album, it didn't find the financial success he had hoped for, so he ended up spending much more money than he made. He was disappointed and angry. *What went wrong*, he wondered? Why did the universe not support him and make him famous?

Can you spot his agenda? His conditioning had co-opted his authentic life purpose and blended it with an egoic desire for external gain. He thought, *I am authentically following my life purpose, therefore I will be recognized and rewarded*. If you think others will recognize you as having accomplished something and flock to you just because you have discovered your true nature and correctly followed your life impulse, think again. Using your spiritual insight for personal gain is an agenda.

Fast forward a few years. Another musician who wrote and sang uplifting songs was at a large meditation retreat I was attending. He sang a few songs for us. It was clear he was simply shining his light because he was so authentically present and evidently delighted at being able to share his passion with us all. There was no sales pitch, no agenda, and I immediately went home and downloaded his album, as I'm sure many other participants did. When we follow the impulse because that's just what we do, others will either be attracted to us or they won't be attracted to us, and either way it is not really any of our business.

When you begin to see your life purpose clearly, you will see the impulse always expresses *as service*. All the good in this world is pioneered by people who have authentically followed their life force. They do so with strong, unwavering purpose. When you watch them work, there is a joyfulness and enthusiasm in what they do. They tend to be energized rather than drained by their work. When you are in flow as life, there is no energetic stress. There is no indecision or stressing about what to do next. Decisions come in the right time, next steps unfold organically, support arrives when required. Life is being lived fully. Living life fully and joyfully does not mean you will be rich and famous! But it does mean you will affect people positively, and your light and joy will ignite something in them and perhaps give them permission to find their inner light too.

Shine Your Big, Bright Light

If you are looking for success in Reiki, as a Reiki teacher or practitioner, it is not based on how hard you work, how many social media followers you have, or how many certificates adorn your wall. People are attracted to your light. The light of your being shines through when you are authentically connected to your true nature. People respond to this and want the same for themselves. When you are doing your Reiki practice, it shows. Have you seen your big, bright light for yourself? If you cannot see it, it will be almost impossible for others to see it too, because you are keeping it hidden under your egoic conditioning.

When you acknowledge your true self and shine your light outwards it is almost like you are a walking Reiki attunement. Your true self resonates with others' true self and allows others to acknowledge that part in them too. This is really what I mean when I said earlier in the book that one person can affect one hundred others. We can have an enormous impact on others simply through our own discovery of our true nature.

If you are wondering why others don't see your potential, or why others are not attracted to what you are offering, is it because you yourself have not seen your own potential? Take the time to find out what you are hiding. And what you are hiding behind!

What attracts you to others? Is it the certificates on their wall, or is it an altogether different quality of trust and authenticity that you yourself look for in others? Whatever you look for in others, make sure you are providing it first.

Years ago, I used to live in New York City on the Upper East Side of Manhattan. We had impeccable doormen there, just like in the movies. They knew our names, went above and beyond their jobs, and they were just amazing. During the blackout of summer 2006, one of them carried my two-year-old daughter up eleven flights of steps because the lifts were out and she was exhausted. This is life purpose in action. Life bursts out cleanly as love, compassion, and enthusiasm. When you're operating out of your true self, every action has meaning and purpose. Every incident is filled with sacred intention and service.

Years later, I was giving an attunement, and I had the most bizarre image of myself as a doorman. All I had to do was open the door wide with love and integrity. My purpose became clear to me at that moment: I was to open the door to Reiki to anyone who wanted to step through it. And that was all I needed to do. I was filled with relief because, after years of practice, attunements are the one thing I can do well!

Life only wants from you what you can freely give. There is no other demand than to do what you naturally love to do. Simply practice and master your craft and shine your light for the benefit of others, that is all. Isn't that wonderful?

Whatever your craft, perfect it. Do it over and over and create a daily practice of it.

If you are a Reiki teacher, every day create a sacred space, centre yourself with a *gassho* (the Japanese word for hands in prayer pose, meaning "uniting palms"), or whatever ritual gesture you personally hold dear, and then practice the attunement on yourself.

Do it with significance, and with sacred intention. This attunement is stepping into the universal life force. This attunement is shining your big, bright light. Do it with intention, sincerity, and integrity. Do it daily and see how it changes your life and transforms your Reiki teaching and ability to attract new students. The more you practice your Reiki in all its forms the more you yourself become a walking Reiki advertisement.

Whatever your life purpose is, whatever direction you feel yourself moving in, understand your part in the greater whole and add value to it. Express your purpose clearly and without conditions, do not dilute or diminish it. In this way, you come into service of life.

Your prosperity is not dependent on what you do, but on how much enthusiasm you have for what you do, how committed you are to the mastery of your craft, and how prepared you are. When you interpret the impulse correctly, you will be in full and enthusiastic co-operation with the universe. You will want to improve things, you will want to leave a legacy—and not for the sake of your inflated ego, but because you see the value in leaving the world in better shape than when you found it in whatever small way you can.

Building on What You Were Given

Life wants to evolve. This is the impulse. Just look at nature, science, the expansion of the universe. Consider what you want to leave, consider the quality of the output of your life. Consider what you want to stand for. Building on what you were given is a growth mentality and comes from an impulse to expand and make things better. It comes from having a clear and open mind. A constricted ego looks for what it can get from life, not what it can give, which is why it is so important to uncover your inner light. When we are living in ego, we are always trying to get things, protect things, keep things. It is very constricted and often unpleasant energy. We can see where it leaves us in the world we have created together. When we work to uncover our inner truth and light our curiosity and focus shifts to what life itself is calling forth through us.

It is not a struggle to be yourself. In fact, it is the easiest, most natural thing in the world. You are simply building on what you already love to do, what you value, what is natural for you. What is your passion?

If you are reading this as a Reiki teacher, I hope you consider the legacy you wish to leave. How do you want to support Reiki, support your students, support the greater good? Be what you want to see, expand the Reiki practice and the spiritual growth and the momentum of our sacred energy. As teachers, we have a responsibility to pass on a deep, strong form of Reiki not a more diluted form. It is up to each of us individually to decide what we want to do and how to go about it.

In whatever field you are in, is your work adding to or degrading the morphic field of your profession? I make it a point to read Reiki books regularly and to listen to other teachers, read blogs, and keep up to date on developments. This is professional but it also opens your mind and keeps you growing. It is what would be expected of anyone in any other field.

If you cannot be a good student, how can you be a good teacher?

When you look at your own material and manuals, how much effort do you put into their ongoing development? Does your manual evolve with you? If your manual has not changed in the past few years, you may want to consider why. Reiki teaching is evolving as Reiki is evolving, and as all the lineages grow, there is more depth and more insight to be delivered. Keeping your materials reflective of your growth as a teacher also helps you to see if your own deepening has stalled and perhaps needs a little kick up the butt.

The Co-Creative Process

It is very hard to articulate the balance required for this stage of spiritual development. I can only say balance comes with experience and practice. I realise that what I am offering here sounds like a fairly typical to-do list for how to become excellent at something. I'm saying practice your craft, become knowledgeable and expert, and walk your talk.

What I really want to clearly communicate is the importance of doing this out of an *authentic* sense of purpose. These steps happen because we feel the importance of them ourselves, and so we have a passion for taking these steps in a natural and effortless way.

When I worked in market research I also knew that in order to be excellent, to get a promotion, to climb the ladder, I needed to get better at doing what I was doing, to learn more and keep abreast of developments in my industry, to take an interest—but I just couldn't do it. I wasn't motivated—there was no driving impulse of life coming out of me for this particular pathway.

With Reiki I want to share, I want to learn, I feel extremely motivated, and I show up decade after decade with joy and gratitude. The difference is not in *what* you are doing, it is in how *aligned* you are with what you are doing. Your abundance comes from the light, passion, and exuberance you shine outwards, because it is contagious!

People look at me with stunned disbelief when I tell them that I can show up month after month and teach the same series of classes again and again. I love it more than words can say! The impulse to share Reiki has been strong all these years, and teaching Reiki is beyond fulfilling for me.

Yet I only consciously saw this in degrees. Way back when I studied at Level 2, the impulse switched on. I was caught by Reiki and the dance began. But I didn't know it to nearly the extent I do today. I travelled the stages I have been describing in this book time and time again always getting more clarity, cleaning up my belief structures, teaching Reiki with joy for sure, but not fully embodying what was happening.

The impulse I felt was mistaken for 101 other things. For example, I mistook the impulse as signifying I had a "lack" time and time again, which spurred me to get training in lots of other healing modalities, embellish my classes, teach all kinds of other topics. I stopped teaching, started again, did healing, stopped again. Struggled over and over, overthought things over and over, and made life so much more difficult than it was. And then at some point, it just became self-evident: *Ah! Teaching Reiki is life's purpose for me!*

It sounds ridiculous, but that's the way of it. You see it when you see it.

I say this to reassure you. You may be reading this final chapter with frustration. You may not have fully aligned with your life purpose yet or you may think you are not living it at all. Rest assured that all your life is, in fact, your purpose, not one bit is wasted, wrong, or mistaken. Hard as that might be to consider, it is the truth. Your life purpose is always shining out of you. Your impulse for creation is always present.

Yes, you may think it's an impulse for cake—easy mistake—but even in that eating of the cake there is a fulfilment of purpose. Just keep clearing the way, deepening your journey, connecting with your true self, until one day you'll see that you can eat cake, *or* you can do something else with the impulse. You will see that the impulse is actually a calling for joy and abundance to shine out of you. And when you see that, then you'll shine.

The beauty of realizing that you are just the dance is that you realise nothing you do is ever wasted or wrong. You are creating as life, not as something separate from it. Your life has equal value whichever path you ultimately choose, and there is no judgment from life about the merits of any particular path. Today, my life purpose is to write and publish this book and teach Reiki. Next year, it may be to become a cashier at a supermarket and shine my light to all those who pile their groceries onto my till. It is not in the doing that we have a fulfilling life; it is in the being. You can have an equally large impact as a cashier as you can a Reiki teacher. You can have an equally miserable life too. It's all up to you.

You can follow the impulse to its largest expression, or you can sit at home and eat cake. This is the nature of the free will we have: to fully open and let life out or be ruled by our fears and insecurities. As life, we enjoy it all fully, whether it is insecurity or whether it is abundance.

Ironically, the more you understand this, the more you are likely to choose abundance. The clearer you see your impulse, the more purpose, direction, and passion flow out of you and into the world.

All most of us have to work on is the inward journey and heightening our sensitivity about where life is heading. What is the impulse that is coming up from deep within your heart? This is the magical dance of life. First, see the light within, then follow its direction. Your bigger purpose is to see that you are the dance, and to give yourself fully to this realization and dance.

10.
In the End

I saw mountains as mountains, and waters as waters. When I arrived at a more intimate knowledge, I came to the point where I saw that mountains are not mountains, and waters are not waters. But now that I have got its very substance I am at rest. For it's just that I see mountains once again as mountains, and waters once again as waters.

—Ch'ing-yüan Wei-hsin

This is such a wonderful quote! I chose it to end this book as it describes the essence of the progression of understanding our true nature. We journey in circles! Before we begin the Reiki journey, we see the world as it is: Mountains are mountains. Waters are waters. We see our place in the world as individual and separate. However, we are suffering because of our beliefs about our separateness. We are suffering because we think the mountains or waters are in the wrong place, or because we envy that others have bigger mountains and more water than we do, or because we feel we are not deserving enough to have mountains and waters, or for reasons acquainted with other types of mental contraction. Then we come to Reiki. It calls us, and somewhere inside us, we heed the call and begin our journey along the Reiki path.

As we embrace the Reiki journey, we come into greater awareness of the magical quality of life. We question everything and see that nothing is as it appears. We are deluded under layers and layers of conditioning, and we need to free ourselves in order to live as life intended. The freedom we seek is within us, so the very first step is to direct our attention away from the glitter and drama of the outside world, and into the wisdom that resides within us.

Turning our attention inward, we come into more intimate and honest connection with our inner world. The body never lies and is the barometer of how life is flowing through us. When we are open and flowing with life's impulse, our bodies reflect this, they are still and peaceful, they are undisturbed. Coming into a deeper sensitivity with your body allows you to tap into a great source of inner truth—it is your early warning signal.

The Reiki self-treatment naturally draws you inwards. It is a tool of unprecedented power. It not only calms and heals the body, but more importantly puts you into direct contact with your inner life. With an intentioned and deliberate practice of inquiry, we aim to combine self-treatment with an alert mind. When we reside in peace and harmony, we notice it, thinking, *This is my true nature. This is who I truly am: peace, love, timeless eternity.* Listening to the body and feeling when it is out of harmony, we learn to bring all rejected parts of ourselves back in, we create acceptance of ourselves, and we begin the journey to self-love. Mastery of this stage, of turning our attention inwards, comes with total self-acceptance and deep respect for the body and its role as our barometer.

In the beginning, we will be faced with many fears as we see all the discomfort, stuffed trauma, and unheard parts of ourselves arise. All I can hope is that you persevere, because the light at the end of the tunnel is bright and steady and beautiful. The more you look, the easier it gets to reach it. The more you look, the less you fear. And the more you look, the lighter and more joyful you become.

Clearing and acceptance open us to the second stage, deconditioning our minds. Our egos are simply contracted and believed thoughts that have created layers around the essence that dwells within us. Sometimes the layers are so thick and contracted that we can barely see our own light. But as you work with Reiki, you will notice it begins to peek through.

When we begin to send Reiki to intention and to unblocking resistance, we first notice how full of agendas we are. The ego wants so much! It says: *I want this and that. People must be like this or that. I want people to do this or that.* The ego makes a series of never-ending demands on us—it's no wonder we are exhausted! At this stage, we notice that these demands do not come from outside. It is not the horrendous mother-in-law after all! We are doing all this to ourselves! We see that we demand and harass ourselves more than our worst enemies. But little by little, the Reiki sending and healing chips away at our conditioning and it begins to loosen up. Just like the body, it opens and releases its contractions.

We become more curious as the mind opens. When we are not constantly bombarded with mental noise, we notice a growing quiet awareness. In between the thoughts, in the gaps, resides a deep presence.

As we focus more and more on the quietness, we become aware of this truth: *I am separate when I bring my attention to my thoughts, and I am oneness when I bring my attention to the gaps.* Depending on where we place our focus, we see we are life itself peering out of our eyes, or we are separated by the narrative of our thoughts, one step removed from reality.

This point of recognition is the height of realizing that all is not as it seems. Some people come to this point with a flash of insight, but for most of us, it is a gradual awakening into the truth of who we really are. It dawns on us: *Reiki and I are one and the same thing. And Reiki and I are separate. There is no conflict; it is simply a point of attention.*

Once you know this, you begin to take more care regarding where you are placing your attention, and magically, mountains and waters come back into focus. The ordinariness of life becomes self-evident again. You may have the unspoken sense: *It has always been like this. It will always be like this. It is exactly as it is.* As the clarity comes through, you see life exactly as it is.

Specifically, you know: *There are layers of conditioned thoughts that I think of as "me," there is perfection in who I am that includes these layers, and there is absolutely nothing to change. Everything is in its perfect place. Everything is exactly as it was when I began my Reiki journey, minus the suffering.* How funny is that?

Having reached this moment, now we see ourselves and life more clearly. Now we can live our life purpose cleanly and without misinterpretation. Life's impulse to dance and experience can be fully felt. Our life purpose has always been there, trying to break out of the layers of our conditioning to shine its light. It feels vibrant and exciting and joyful. Now we can feel life in all its glory and see it everywhere, bursting out of flowers, radiating out of trees, dancing in the eyes of everyone we meet. So much abundance and love and energy that it's extraordinary we ever missed it, because it is so evident. We enjoy this amazing display of life in everything we do, and we realise that this is our life purpose—to fully love life and honour what the universe has created. It is astounding and magnificent.

In the end, we come back to the beginning. The mountains and waters are back in focus, we see them clearly without the layers of conditioned narrative that separates us from them. We experience them with all our senses, there is no suffering, there is just pure perfection. And as we gaze, fully absorbed, that little conditioned ego nudges us *oy, snap out of it! Dinner isn't going to make itself stupid!*

Postlude

Next Steps

I am reluctant to present you with a how-to list for your Reiki practice, as in my experience, people invariably will turn such a list into a burdensome set of must-dos, which is not the point of this book at all. To the contrary, developing a personalized self-treatment regimen is ultimately what I wish for you. But despite my reluctance, I know starting points are helpful. Therefore, I am presenting you with a few suggestions here because I suspect that you may not be taking into consideration the discipline required to follow this path at the beginning.

Reiki will move you inwards. If you practice your Reiki mindfully, you will see quicker results than if you use your self-treatments to zone out mentally. The list that follows is designed to give you an indication of what is required from you as a Reiki student, so that you don't delude yourself that reading this book, then going about your daily life, is going to do anything much for you. The truth is that most of us are stuck in our habits and conditioning and it takes dedication and a huge amount of energy to break free.

Ideally, your Reiki spiritual practice should include the following elements.

Self-treatment. I am sure this is obvious by now. The key to unlocking inner joy and freedom begins with regular self-treatment.

Personally, I recommend doing a full hour of treatment daily, but any amount of dedicated and deliberate practice is better than nothing. Start wherever you are and build upwards, timewise, from there.

Remember also that during your practice, where you place your attention is key. You are looking inwards with the intent of getting to know more about your body and inner life; you are not daydreaming or sorting out dinner plans.

The use of symbols. The Reiki symbols are packed with power and information that will aid you in your spiritual exploration. Bring these tools into play throughout the day, for example by harmonising and empowering everything and everyone—become a walking Reiki emitter. Radiate the symbols out into the world and throughout your environment. By stepping into their morphic fields every day, many times a day, you are inviting their power to merge more and become integrated with your personal energy field, and this will have a significant impact on releasing your conditioning.

Sending. I cannot emphasize how powerful it is to send Reiki to your life challenges. As a daily morning practice, I wake up, make myself a cup of coffee, and then spend ten minutes journaling and reflecting on how I'm feeling in general, what is troubling me, and what I would like to bring more of into my life. I write a label (a sentence in my journal that summarises my priority for the day) stating either an intention or my desire to release a contracted belief or obstacle, and then I send Reiki to it for fifteen minutes. For example, a label could read "I trust in the flow of life," if I am finding trust particularly difficult one day, or "How do I shift my thinking about this issue?" if I am struggling with something specific. As I send Reiki the most profound messages can come up or unfold during the day.

This thirty-minute morning ritual has helped me more than I can tell you as it sets the tone for the rest of the day and often brings deep insight. If it is not feasible to send Reiki every day, make it a weekly practice. Just remember, consistently and deliberately looking at your conditioned programs and algorithms will loosen them up and allow you to see your true light under all the layers.

Attunements (*Reiju*). Making a practice of doing regular attunements (either on yourself or on others) merges you more deliberately with universal life force. Every time you do an attunement, you resonate with your true nature. Each one shakes things up a bit, like a hammer cracking through all the layers of conditioning. Over time your conditioning begins to crack open and you become more and more familiar with your life force.

If you are not able to do attunements yourself, seek out a community or teacher (face to face or online) who is offering them. If you are a teacher, offer heart attunements regularly to your students during your community gatherings or online.

If you incorporate these practices daily or as regularly as possible, you will find that the Reiki path supports you in a natural and inevitable unfolding. The stages I have outlined in this book are a natural progression based on these practices, there is nothing magical about them. It is cause and effect coupled with an unwavering courage and sincerity to look inwards for your truth.

As you continue to journey inwards, you may see an equally important outward by-product developing—the sharing of what you have discovered. If you develop your own regular Reiki practice you will emit more and more Reiki, love and compassion. You will affect people in positive ways simply by being around them.

If this book is a manifesto for anything, it is a call to all Reiki students to shine their lights by coming more consciously and deliberately into their inner freedom and truth. Your one light will ignite a hundred others. And those hundred will ignite another ten thousand. Those ten thousand another million. The truth is, we already have millions of Reiki students on this planet, so together we really could ignite the whole of humanity.

Who is with me?

Wishing you freedom and joy on your Reiki journey.

Elaine

Acknowledgements

This book has been an extraordinary journey. When I first mentioned I was writing it to my long-time friend, Elaine Harris, she laughed and told me I was in for the roller coaster ride of my life. She was not wrong. I had a fairly clear idea of my message at the start, but I look back and see it was really only a seed, and over the past year of evolution it has grown into a little seedling and continues to grow.

I am grateful to the amazing tribe of women who sprang up around me to nurture this transition: to the Elaines, my UK tribe–Katherine, Sally, Jemma, Debra, Lesley, Jane—and my Singapore tribe–Karen, Chris, Clarice, Julie Ann, Ashley. To the incredible Reiki master community, thank you for your love, support, and amazing work. To One Heart, Jas and Simon, who allow me to call their lovely Centre home.

For their assistance in putting this book together, I need to thank Hilary Galea for setting me on the right path and Stephanie Gunning for her exceptional editing skills, patience, and humour—your description of Takata will be forever my favourite. To Justine Elliott for another great book cover and design—you did it again! To Gauri, Karen, and Elaine for reading the many versions of this book and encouraging me onwards. To all those who supported the

Kickstarter campaign and showed me so much support and love—I am so grateful.

The more I deepen my own journey with Reiki the more I realise the incredible depth of my own training, and for that I am eternally grateful to my Reiki teachers, John and Esther Veltheim and René Vögtli, for igniting the Reiki flame in me.

Finally, I am grateful to my wonderful family—Ella and Holly, Roger and Martin, Ian, and my mum and dad. You all inspire me to be a better version of myself daily.

With enormous gratitude to the following people:

Adrienne Kouwenhoven
Alice Dantin Perkins
Angie Nguyen Anh Thu
Ann Lee
Anne Marie Brooks
Anne Perng
Anson
Au Kee Hin
Ayisha F.D.
Brenda Chou
Burçin Gezer
Chris Angus
Christine Brække
Christine Vavra
Clare Chiang
Clarice Chan
Dani Van de Velde
Danny Dewulf
Darvinya Paramesvaran
Dawn Chan
Cathy Ripley Greene
Eckshar Isis
Elaine Victoria Yang
Gauri Ramirez
Gitta Van Roy
Hilary Lee
Janice Goh
Jaslyn Kee-Ng
Jennifer Dunbar
Joanne Thia
Jorva and Neil Hamilton
Julie Ann Gledhill
Justin Saw
JY Chan
Karen C.
Karen Taylor
Karthigayan Kandavellu
Katherine
Katherine Lee
Kim Wesseler
Kunadoobie Lindsay
Leslie Modell
Lies Dekeyser
Lim Shin, Zhixin
Mabel Yap
Malene Bloch Lundgaard
Martin Sisiak
Meenakshi Sarup
Michele Fernyhough
Miki

Ming Li Tan
Nelly
Niki
Pallavi Desai
Patricia Leong
Patricia Thompson RMT
Pauline Teo
Pooja Arora
Pooja Chugh
Raymond Kua Joo Siang
Rie Komiya
Rika Dwi Laksanti
Rochelle
Roger Swee
Roopa
Sarah Deeks
Sarah Lees
Serene Koh
Serene Tan
Shirley Hill Maljanen
Silpa Shah
Simon Kee
Simrin Gregory
Sowmya Subramanian
Swati Sood
Tekai Law
Tharanga Gamage
Wang Yng
Wehda El Aridi
Wei Shimin
Wendy Kuest
Yan Yoke Ming
ZiHu
And others.

Notes

Prelude: Learning to Unlearn
Epigraph. Byron Katie. *A Mind at Home with Itself* (New York: HarperCollins, 2017), p.197.

Introduction
Epigraph. Adyashanti. *The End of Your World* (Boulder, Colorado: Sounds True, 2010), p.42.

Chapter 1: Universal Life Force
Epigraph. Richard Feynman. *The Feynman Lectures on Physics, Volume 3* (Boston, MA.: Addison-Wesley, 1965), pp. 18–9.

Chapter 2: A Finger Pointing to the Moon
Epigraph. Osho. *Zarathustra: A God That Can Dance* (Zurich, CH.: Osho International, 2012), p.219.
1. Ibid., p. 220.
2. John Veltheim, from my personal notes taken during Reiki Level 1 class (Hong Kong, 1992).

Chapter 3: Understanding the Reiki Symbols
Epigraph. J.C. Cooper. *An Illustrated Encyclopaedia of Traditional Symbols* (London, U.K.: Thames & Hudson, 1987), p. 7.

1. Rupert Sheldrake. "Morphic Resonance," Rupert Sheldrake (accessed September 28, 2019), https://www.sheldrake.org/research/morphic-resonance.
2. Rupert Sheldrake. *The Presence of the Past: Morphic Resonance and the Memory of Nature* (Rochester, N.Y.: Park Street Press, 2012), p. 218.

Chapter 4: Reiki Attunements for Personal Growth
Epigraph. Frans Stiene. *The Inner Heart of Reiki* (Abingdon, U.K.: Ayni Books, 2014), p. 118.

Chapter 5: Reiki as a Spiritual Practice
Epigraph. Frank Arjava Petter. *Reiki Fire: New Information about the Origins of the Reiki Power* (Twin Lakes, WI.: Lotus Press, 1997), p. 28.
1. John and Esther Veltheim. *Reiki: The Science, Metaphysics, and Philosophy* (Union Hall, VA.: PaRama, 1995), p. 8.
2. Ibid., p. 71.
3. Ibid., p. 143.
4. Gasser, R.; Veigl, L. "Effect of Meditation upon Arterial Blood Pressure," *Journal of Hypertension*, vol. 35, e-supplement 2 (September 2017), p. e298.
5. Richard Rivard. *The Usui Reiki Ryoho Gakkai Handbook* (Vancouver, CA.: Reiki Threshold, 2007), p. 4.
6. Tweet from Deepak Chopra (25 May 2013), www.Twitter.com/DeepakChopra.

Chapter 6: Turning Attention Inwards
Epigraph. Maya Angelou, from an interview in *USA Today* (5 March 1988).

Chapter 7: Deconditioning the Mind
Epigraph. Eckhart Tolle. *Stillness Speaks* (London, U.K.: Hodder and Stoughton, 2003), p. 34.

Chapter 8: Minding the Gap
Epigraph. Thich Nhat Hanh, from an interview in O, *The Oprah Magazine* (March 2010), http://www.oprah.com/spirit/oprah-talks-to-thich-nhat-hanh/2.

Chapter 9: Living Life's Purpose
Epigraph. Eckhart Tolle. *A New Earth: Awakening to Your Life's Purpose* (London, U.K.: Penguin Books, 2005). p. 115.

Chapter 10: In the End
Epigraph. Ch'ing-yüan Wei-hsin, as cited by Alan Watts. *The Way of Zen* (New York: Pantheon, 1957), p. 126.

About the Author

Elaine Grundy is a Reiki master teacher and founder of the Reiki Centre. She became a Reiki teacher in 1995. She has introduced many thousands of students to Reiki and over eighty Reiki teachers have been through her vigorous 200-hour mastery program. Her first book *Reiki, Pure and Simple* was published in 2010 and serves as a down to earth introduction to Reiki.

Elaine has lived and taught all around the world including Hong Kong, Malaysia, Singapore, Portugal, the United Kingdom and the United States of America.

Elaine offers the spiritual path of Reiki as a doorway to greater self-awareness. Through her writing and videos, she hopes to convey the important message that we all have the capacity to wake up to our true nature and experience life to its full potential. Her online webinars and courses give Reiki students an opportunity to dive deeper.

Elaine provides virtual teaching and individual mentoring. She enjoys traveling and assisting Reiki communities deepen their Reiki tools through her talks, workshops and retreats. For more information please visit: www.Reiki-Centre.com

Printed in Great Britain
by Amazon